BUSINESS STRATEGY & PLANNING

Edited by Bernard Taylor

Inflation and business policy

D. E. Hussey

Longman
London and New York

Longman Group Limited London

Associated companies, branches and representatives throughout the world

Published in the United States of America by Longman Inc., New York

First published 1976

Library of Congress Cataloging in Publication Data

Hussey, David E.
Inflation and business policy.

(Business strategy and planning)
Includes bibliographical references and index.
1. Industrial management and inflation. 2. Inflation (Finance) I. Title.
HD69.I6H87 658.1'552 76-7065
ISBN 0 582 45073 X

Set in IBM Century 10 on 12pt
and printed in Great Britain by
Lowe and Brydone (Printers) Ltd,
Thetford, Norfolk

Contents

Acknowledgements

We are grateful to the following for permission to reproduce copyright material:

The author for an extract from an unpublished paper 'Note on the scope for improved productivity in industry' by Norman Dudley; George Allen and Unwin Ltd, for an extract from *Managing the Multinationals* by Business International. Published by George Allen and Unwin Ltd; Associated Business Programmes Ltd, for extracts from *The United Kingdom in 1980: The Hudson Report* by the Hudson Institute Europe, published by the Associated Business Programmes, London, 1974; Conference Board Record for two extracts from 'Inflation: Impact on consumer attitudes and behaviour' by G. Katona in *Containing Inflation in the 1970s*, M. E. Levy (ed.), 1971; The Controller of Her Majesty's Stationery Office for an extract from *Price Adjustment Formulae for Building Contracts* and for a table from the *Department of Employment Gazette*, May 1975; The Institute of Chartered Accountants in England and Wales for extracts from *Accounts for Changes in the Purchasing Powers of Money: Proposed Statement of Intended Accounting Practice*, 1973; National Association of Lift Makers for an extract from 'Formula for contract price adjustment in respect of variation in costs'; National Institute of Economic and Social Research for two tables from the *National Institute Economic Review*, May 1975; Royal Institute of British Architects for Clauses from the 'Standard form of building contract'; Director Publications Ltd, for a diagram showing the prices of three key commodities from *The Director*, January 1974; The London School of Economics and Political Science for a table from Phelps Brown and Hopkins' article in *Economica*, November 1956; Pergamon Press Ltd, for a figure from *Corporate Planning: Theory and Practice* by the author, published by Pergamon, 1974, and for a diagram from *Strategic Planning for Resources* by B. Taylor. Published by Pergamon, 1974; Penguin Books Ltd, for a figure from *An Insight into Management Accounting* by J. Sizer. Published by Penguin, 1969, Professor B. J. Lalonde for an article published in *The Journal of Business Policy*, Spring 1972.

We regret that we have been unable to trace the copyright holder of tables from *Managing the Multinationals* by Business International. Published by George Allen and Unwin Ltd.

Introduction

Surprisingly little has been written from a management point of view to help those concerned with the running of businesses to evaluate and counter the effects of inflation on their activities. There have, of course, been many studies of the economic/political aspects of inflation but these are usually written from a macro-economic viewpoint. Recently attention has been paid to finance, with the emphasis being on inflation accounting. There have also been some writings on labour relations, but again most of these take a national stand and gloss over the problems of the individual firm.

Inflation has been a matter of general concern for many years. Despite this, it has rarely been seen as a matter with specific implications for the running of a business. Failure to think about inflation at this level was a fault found throughout business, until we all came face to face with reality in the shape of the world hyperinflation which arrived with the events at the end of 1973 and early 1974. The energy crisis, rising commodity prices, and the revolt against Government wage restraints which led to the three-day week in the UK have brought an awareness which has meant a rude awakening for those who previously dismissed inflation as unimportant.

Opinion has changed. In May 1974 I organised a conference for the Society for Long-Range Planning on inflation and its impact on corporate strategy. Applications flooded in, the event was over-subscribed, and some of those interested could not be given places. Yet only a year earlier what was substantially the same conference had had to be cancelled through lack of support. All that had changed in the intervening period was that more people had become aware that inflation has a considerable effect on their businesses.

Inflation is by no means a new phenomenon, and something of its history is traced later in this book. Recent years have shown that it has increased its intensity as a problem, and it now assumes a form which must taint almost every element of business. It is an issue which has widespread implications for policies and strategies in all business functions: marketing, production, purchasing, finance, industrial relations and manpower. It is also international in scope and a factor in changing the relative competitive positions not only of companies but also of nations.

The aim of this book is to help all those concerned with business policy to add to their understanding of the impact of inflation on their businesses, and to identify positive actions which they might take to avoid its problems and to benefit from its opportunities.

This is an ambitious objective, and in attempting to attain it I have concentrated on the practical rather than the theoretical, both because I believe that this is what managers most need and because my own exposure to inflation has been in a working situation as a manager in industry. So although the book draws on the works of others, and could not have been written without doing so, much also comes from approaches I have found useful in a working situation.

As a practising corporate planner I have long had a general concern with inflation and its effects on strategy, and have given some attention to the problem in my books on corporate planning. Yet it was only in 1970 that I came to a realisation of the true size of the problem, when the company which employed me was faced with severe increases in the costs of all its major raw materials (one doubled in price over twelve months).

There is nothing like a 100 per cent cost rise to focus the mind, and since 1970 inflation has rarely been out of any thoughts I have had on business planning and strategy. What I faced in 1970 was no more than the rude awakening which other types of business had to come to terms with some four to five years later, and my main ability to produce this book derives from the longer period I have had to learn from the experience.

The first four chapters explore the major implications of inflation and hyperinflation, and argue the case for urgent action by all managers. The remainder of the book deals more specifically with the nature of the action which should be considered. Lest any of the recommendations be lost in the detail of the argument, the last chapter presents an action summary.

This has not been an easy book to write, partly because the subject is so vast, and partly because it deals with topical affairs, which have a habit of changing. As a subject it trespasses on disciplines which include those of the economist, planner, accountant, psychologist, sociologist, and statistician. The fact that the economic and social scene is constantly moving means that it is easy for the book to become out of date before it has even been completed. While this is unimportant to most of the recommendations, it does complicate some of the analysis. It is for this reason that I decided against including a chapter on Government anti-inflation policies, since I felt that the reader would obtain a more up-to-date view from his daily newspaper than from a book which is likely to lag twelve months from the writing of the final word to actual publication.

Because the subject is so broad, no one writer can ever do justice to it. A secondary aim of the book is to stimulate others to turn their minds to the problem. It is an area which requires both thought and action on the part of managers, for if we can neither overcome inflation nor learn to profit from it we are left with only a very insecure future ahead of us.

The more I worry about the issues, the more I see to worry about. In many ways I feel in the same position as Tolkien's artist, Niggle, whose attempts to paint a leaf led him to a realisation that he was tackling only a very small part of the real picture (Tolkien, 1974).*

> There was one picture in particular which bothered him. It had begun with a leaf caught in the wind, and it became a tree; and the tree grew, sending out innumerable branches, and thrusting out the most fantastic roots. Strange birds came and settled on the twigs and had to be attended to. Then all round the tree, and behind, through gaps in the leaves and boughs, a country began to open out; and there were glimpses of a forest marching over the land, and of mountains topped with snow.

I see the problem as serious, and many of the possible directions which our future can take fill me with the deepest concern. Yet I do not think this is in any way a pessimistic book, for there is much that every manager can do to manage and control his business even under the most acute conditions of hyperinflation. The important thing is to tackle the problem head on, to take positive action, to work on the issue. No manager can afford to abdicate, or to sit passively waiting for events to overwhelm him.

I hope this book makes some contribution, however small, to the action that must be taken. It may only be one leaf out of the total picture, but even the most complex of solutions to the most complex of problems has to have a starting point somewhere.

My thanks are due to Professor Bernard Taylor of the Administrative Staff College, Henley-on-Thames, who discussed the synopsis of the book with me at some length, and to the many other people who have allowed me to quote from their work.

The typing of a book is always a major undertaking. My thanks go to Mrs S. E. Webb, who translated my handwriting into a readable manuscript. As much of the book was written on innumerable train journeys this was no mean achievement.

* References are positioned at the end of chapters.

Reference

Tolkien, J. R. (1964) 'Leaf by Niggle', *Tree and Leaf*, Allen and Unwin, p. 73.

1

The problem of inflation

In recent years inflation, as an issue, has taken up a good deal of the time of economists, journalists and politicians. It has played its part in changing the popularity of political parties, for the remedies applied by successive governments have been no more liked than the ills they are meant to heal. The majority of voters are opposed both to the disease and the various cures which have been tried from time to time.

Surprisingly, inflation as a specific business problem — or more exactly a host of related problems — has received much less attention. Of course it has been a factor which managers have considered in relation to their day-to-day problems. It has arisen in wage negotiations, pricing decisions and through the need to comply with the anti-inflation regulations which may from time to time have been in force. It has been of vital concern to undertakings which have long-term contracts as a feature of their business; hence the price variation, or escalation, clauses which are basic to industries such as construction.

Business can by no means be accused of having ignored the issue of inflation. It can, as a generalisation, be indicted for treating it as a short-term tactical issue rather than one of longer term strategic importance. In fact interest in inflation in a significant number of companies rarely moves to the strategic level. Many managers will openly state that inflation is not considered an important factor in their business plans and is generally ignored. The validity of this step rests on three major assumptions:

1 That cost increases will always be recovered by price increases;
2 That inflation has no effect on the shape or size of markets;
3 That relative competitive positions remain unaffected as inflation hits all companies in an industry with the same impact.

It would indeed be very pleasant if these assumptions were true. Unfortunately they are not and, because they are not, inadequate attention to inflation can result in poor decisions or missed opportunities.

In these days of Government interest in and regulation of prices the first assumption is patently untrue. In fact it has always been untrue, since business generally tends to adjust prices some time after cost increases are felt, and in many cases has to consider competitive activity and the state of the market before acting. The growth of any particular market cannot be treated as if prices are constant, but must also be related to the changing incomes of consumers, the relative price of substitutes, and the psychology of the consumer: his perception of what he is willing to pay for a particular item. Inflation does not treat companies fairly, so relative competitive positions can change, particularly under modern conditions of increased international competition in many markets. The impact of inflation varies — from country to country, from industry to industry, from company to company within each industry. The individual firm may improve its competitive position, decline, or stay the same. Its productivity is unlikely to be identical to that of other firms in the industry, it may use different processes of manufacture, process different raw materials and have a different overhead structure.

It is the fact that inflation is unequal in its effects which makes it an important area of business policy. Many companies have the ability to take actions which will reduce the impact on them of inflation. In some cases the effects can be avoided, in others they can be mitigated and in any case the new sets of circumstances will bring a pattern of opportunities which may be lost to the company which takes the ostrich's approach to the problem.

The fact that inflation is frequently a corporate blind spot is typified by the way in which many businesses treat purchases. Raw materials, supplies and services are dangerous carriers of the inflation disease. Where there is a production process between purchasing and selling, procurement is rarely considered a matter for strategic concern, and the purchasing function is often seen as an adjunct of production. Few companies research the markets where they purchase with anything like the thoroughness with which they study the markets where they sell. Purchasing research and planning units, such as that operated by Ciba-Geigy (UK) Ltd are something of a rarity. There are comparatively few firms where the buyer has a place in the top management circle.

Retailing and wholesaling tend to be a little different because the marketing and purchasing decisions are very closely related. Businesses which rely on one or two major commodities, such as oil, may also take a different view. But the vast majority of companies, purchasing a wide variety of raw materials, components and supplies, seem to organise themselves in such a way that the intrusion of procurement into the strategic planning process is a virtual impossibility.

Figure 1.1 shows how, in one company, the costs of its three major

Fig. 1.1 Example of movement in cost of three raw materials

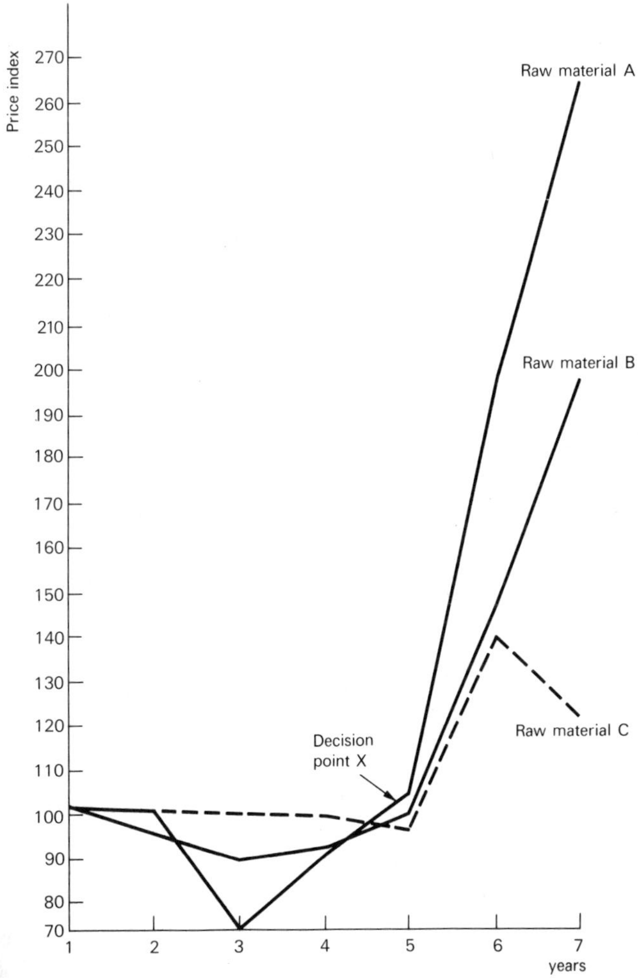

raw materials moved over a period of seven years. The identity of the company, the particular materials and the time span are unimportant, although the indices are drawn from real data.

At point X on the graph the company, looking back over recent history, would have noticed a general declining tendency in each of the three items. Certainly the historic pattern showed no cause for alarm, and could not have led to a forecast of the dramatic increases which were to come. In circumstances like these, the astute buyer with his ear to the ground might well have had an inkling that prices were about to rise. In most companies his chances of inputting an unquantifiable feeling into strategic thinking would have been virtually nil.

In the example, prices rose after point X. At this time the company was giving little attention to studying its supply markets and experienced managers rationalised the increases by arguing that the commodities from which their raw materials were derived did tend to rise every few years, but always went down again after a year. Simple market research was applied, and although this by itself could not provide a forecast of future prices, it demonstrated the fallaciousness of the rationalisation. A series of basic changes had taken place in the supply markets, and for some products a decrease in price was a virtual impossibility and the only one that could decrease would have a future tendency to rise. This knowledge alone helped the company in its forward planning, and to it was added forecasts of raw material prices and analyses of the effect on the company of different levels of raw material, labour and price inflation. The methodology of such an approach is left for later chapters.

Raw-material inflation is of course, only one part of the problem faced by business. Nevertheless, an ability to forecast at point X anything approximating to what actually would happen could lead the company to a number of decision areas which would otherwise be ignored. For example, a company in this situation might:

1 put a new emphasis on research and development to find substitute raw materials, or new processes of manufacture which would lead to a greater economy in the use of the sensitive materials;
2 make a decision to invest in available new technology which would have the same effect: cost savings which might have given too low a return to justify the capital expenditure in the past might well satisfy all financial criteria at the forecast level of prices;
3 re-assess the marketing prospects for the products which would be affected by the massive cost escalation, possibly resulting in the withdrawal of the product, a change in advertising concept, or a reduction (or increase) in promotional expenditure;
4 postpone plans to expand the production of those items under cost pressure, particularly if major investment is required;
5 examine alternative production strategies, perhaps rationalising plants across country borders in order to produce economies of scale, or possibly transferring manufacture from high cost to low cost units in other countries;
6 put a new emphasis on diversification, in order to protect profits and reduce dependence on products whose prospects may be impaired by cost pressures;
7 change purchasing commitments, sources of supply, or methods of purchasing.

It is not only business management which overlooks inflation: the public sector is equally at fault. Corporate plans produced by the Greater London Council have ignored inflation, an approach found in many other local authorities. As local government accounts for more than 10 per cent of gross national expenditure in the UK this cannot be treated as a matter of little significance.

Central government, too, has had its share of failures in inflation calculations. Perhaps one of the most obvious examples is Concorde, the total cost of which has increased many times during the course of the project (Table 1.1). Although the cause of this is usually given as inflation, it is relevant to ask whether other factors, such as the hardening of estimates and design changes, have also played a part.

Table 1.1 Revision to the estimated cost of developing Concorde (£million)

Date of estimate	*Previous estimate*	*Design changes*	*Inflation*	*Other*	*New estimate*
Nov. 1962	—	—	—	—	150—70
July 1964	150—70	45	65	—	275
Mar. 1965	275	—	—	50(*c*)	325
1966	325	←—— 95 ——→		80(*d*)	500
May 1969	450(*a*)	90	150(*b*)	40(*e*)	730
Oct. 1970	730	55	40	—	825
May 1971	825	30	15	15(*c*)	885
May 1972	885	25	60	—	970
June 1973	970	—	75(*b*)	20(*c*)	1,065

Notes: (*a*) 1966 estimate less £50 million contingencies; (*b*) Includes exchange rate changes; (*c*) Cost of postponing certification, which may be inflation; (*d*) Estimate for 'development funding' 1971—73; (*e*) Underestimate of time and effort required — includes some inflation.
Source: British Aircraft Association.

'Inflation' is an overworked word, and the meanings given to it are explored in greater depth in Chapter 2, where the probable causes are examined, although the complexity of the problem is such that it is doubtful whether all the causes are yet known. For the present it may be interpreted as a general condition of rising prices.

One reason why inflation has tended to escape from business attention for so long is that until recently it ran at a tolerable level in the USA and Europe (some figures are discussed later in this chapter). This is not to say that companies would not have benefited by giving it more attention, but it did mean that for most companies inflation was unlikely to cause a disaster of enormous proportions. Certain countries have tended to suffer from acute inflation over long periods. South American countries are well known for rates of inflation varying from 20 to 50 per cent. Indonesia was reported as having made progress in controlling inflation when it fell to 85 per cent in 1968, a great improvement over the 650 per cent only two years before. Similarly, some firms have had higher inflation than others, depending on their unique mix of raw materials and labour, a point which was made earlier in this chapter.

Another reason for lack of concern is the fact that many traditional economics textbooks stress that a reasonable amount of inflation stimulates economic growth. Many of us felt that the inflation we used to experience was reasonable, and that the South American rates could never happen to us. Similarly, few ever contemplated the possibility that we might experience what happened in Germany between January 1913 (when an index of wholesale prices could have been stated as 1) and November 1923 (when it had reached 750,000 million) (Heaton, 1948).

Accounting systems have frequently proved inadequate, in that there are still many companies in which accounting is an exercise for the historian, and too rarely provides a future-oriented view. Purchasing commitments at higher prices may be known somewhere in the company some months before they feed into the Accounts as a variance against standard costs, but are seldom fed into the decision process. Although the concept of inflation accounting is now being adopted (see Chapter 11), this is still new to many businesses, and in any case can only help the company plan for the future by throwing light on a different facet of its past.

Some of the effects of the inflation disease on business were given in the raw material example (Fig. 1.1): the obvious issues of costs, prices and margins; the changing competitive position of firms and nations; the way in which it affects the nature and size of markets. There are others. Inflation can be a great social evil, affecting the standard of living, the expectations and the livelihood of individual people. Because people are purchasers these effects have their impact on markets. Because these same people are for the most part wage earners and their dependants, the problem overflows into industrial relations. Feelings of unfairness and demands for 'social justice' come to the surface. Society's view of profit may change to accusations of profiteering, and in its wake bring new patterns of legislation to control and restrict such 'antisocial' activities.

That inflation can strike at shareholders and corporate growth is clearly demonstrated in the report *Inflation and Company Accounts in Mechanical Engineering* published by the National Economic Development Office, 1973. This study took the published accounts of 126 quoted companies in the mechanical engineering industry whose turnover accounted for about a third of total industry output, and studied the developments over the period 1965—71 on an inflation accounting basis. The normal accounts showed that £124 million were ploughed back into the businesses over the period; that total assets and liabilities increased by 53 per cent; that 1971 profits totalled £159 million; and return on capital employed rose from 12.9 per cent in 1965 to 13.8 per cent in 1971. All accounts prepared on a historic cost basis distorted the real situation, and when these had been adjusted for inflation this distortion became more apparent. In real terms, only £10 million had been retained (not £124 million); total assets and liabilities had increased by only 18 per cent; profits were £30 million lower at £129 million; and return on capital employed slumped to 9.7 per cent. What this study really shows is that the industry was not earning enough to improve its situation under inflationary conditions.

Another aspect of the problem is that in an inflationary situation depreciation allowances are rarely enough to provide for replacement of the assets. Cash flow problems can become more acute, partly because new stocks tend to cost more than those they replace — a problem most readily seen in the case of a small retailer drawing from the cash in the till to replenish his stocks at the local cash-and-carry. Every significant rise in prices means that he has to use more of today's margins to replenish stocks for tomorrow's sale. An additional cash-flow problem is caused by paper profits, brought about for example by stock appreciation.

Inflation makes forward planning of any kind more difficult. It brings a new dimension to studies of future products and markets, and it makes it harder to estimate what the capital requirements of a project will really be: the problem is partly illustrated by the Concorde figures (Table 1.1), and is related to the question of providing adequately for the replacement of assets through depreciation. The impact of the problem can easily be shown by the simple example of the young married couple saving for a house: every time they get together the minimum deposit they find that prices have risen, and that not only do they need a larger deposit but their incomes must also rise if they are to become eligible for the sort of loan they now need. This sort of situation can recur several times — and incidentally also points to yet another of the social ills of inflation. Business is likely to have more flexibility in its solutions than the wouldbe house buyers, but this does not mean the problem can be ignored. Unnecessary delays in making a decision are, in an inflationary situation, likely to be expensive. While careful appraisal is important and should not be skimped, big company bureaucracy should be avoided. It is by no means unknown for large companies to take months — in exceptional cases more than a year — for projects to be approved after evaluation: sometimes the appraisal is done twice, once at subsidiary level and again in head office. Delays are often disadvantageous in business for many reasons: an inflationary situation can make them more costly and still leave all the other disadvantages.

This is by no means a complete analysis of the impact of inflation on business policy, and all the issues discussed are explored in greater depth in later chapters. This preliminary appraisal is designed to show that the issue of inflation should receive more management attention than it has in the past. Such attention is needed because the situation is not all bad. There are actions companies can take, some of which were touched on in the raw material example. Motives for corporate concern with inflation may be self-centred, to ensure that the company continues to develop and prosper despite the threat posed by inflation. At the least this means the maintenance of profits in real terms — that is, after allowing for inflation. More likely it suggests a measure of growth in real profits.

Business also exists as part of society, and although its prime concern is with profit, it also has certain obligations. One of these might well be considered to be to help towards reducing the rate of inflation in the economy at large. This implies a greater understanding of the dynamics of inflation than many companies currently possess, and a commitment to a policy of seeking non-inflationary alternatives when actions to protect profits are being contemplated. If inflation is seen as a strategic problem, and the time horizons for considering it are lengthened, this becomes a realistic and achievable approach. The aim then changes to ensuring that the company develops and prospers, and as far as possible avoids contributing to an increased rate of inflation.

This is a challenge indeed. It is not an easy challenge to meet, but it is my belief that it can be met. The aim of this book is to show that a company facing up to inflation need not be without weapons, for there are many positive actions which can be taken.

So far the scope of the inflation problem has been outlined, but little attempt has been made to define the size of that problem. Table 1.2 examines inflationary trends in various countries by comparing move-

Table 1.2 Consumer price index. Percentage change over previous year

Year	*USA*	*Canada*	*Japan*	*Holland*	*France*	*Germany*	*Italy*	*UK*
1965	1.8	2.5	6.8	5.2	2.5	3.4	4.4	4.6
1966	2.8	3.7	5.1	5.8	2.7	3.5	2.3	3.7
1967	2.9	3.5	4.0	3.2	2.6	1.4	3.3	2.4
1968	4.2	4.2	5.4	3.6	4.6	1.5	1.3	4.8
1969	5.4	4.5	5.2	7.5	6.4	2.7	2.6	5.2
1970	5.9	3.3	7.6	4.4	5.3	3.7	5.0	6.5
1971	4.3	2.9	6.3	7.6	5.5	5.3	5.0	9.5
1972	3.3	4.8	4.9	7.8	5.9	5.5	5.6	6.8
1973	6.2	7.6	11.7	8.0	7.3	6.9	10.4	8.2
1974	11.0	10.9	22.9	9.6	13.7	7.0	19.4	16.0

Source: Derived from figures published in the National Institute of Economic and Social Research, *Economic Review.*

ments in the consumer price index for each year. This is only one of many measures of inflation (Chapter 6 gives more detail on the different measures which may be used), and of course there are always reservations when comparing international statistics. The figures show that there are wide variations in the rate of inflation between one year and the next: the UK for example has a low of 2.4 per cent (1967) and a high of 16 per cent (1974). There are also major differences between countries: for example in 1965 a low 1.8 per cent (USA) compares with a high 6.8 per cent (Japan); in 1971 a low 2.9 per cent (Canada) compares with a high 9.5 per cent (UK). In none of the countries has there been an actual fall in the general level of prices. Whether high or low, the rate of inflation has always shown an increase. Perhaps the most disturbing point is that not only is inflation always with us, but it shows a general tendency to get worse. Any of the rates of inflation shown should be sufficient to cause concern: the higher rates demand positive action.

Table 1.3 Comparison of percentage change in UK retail prices, materials used in manufacture and wholesale prices of manufactured products indices

Monthly averages	*Retail prices*	*Materials used in manufacture*	*Wholesale prices of all manufactured products*
1964	3.9	4.2	2.9
1965	4.6	1.2	3.8
1966	3.7	2.6	2.6
1967	2.4	(1.5)	1.1
1968	4.9	9.0	4.1
1969	5.1	2.2	2.2
1970	6.5	5.3	7.0
1971	9.5	4.6	9.0
1972	6.8	4.4	5.3
1973	8.4	32.1	7.3
1974	15.9	49.0	23.3

Source: Derived from figures published in the National Institute of Economic and Social Research, *Economic Review*.

Table 1.3 shows how changes in the UK retail prices index compares with two other indices which measure inflation. The object here is to demonstrate the point made earlier, that inflation is not one single general factor, smoothed evenly over the economy like butter on bread. Despite the differences in the rates of inflation in these series a general picture of a worsening problem emerges. This is the same conclusion which comes out of a study of the data in Table 1.2. Even comparatively low rates of inflation cumulate to a significant increase in price

Table 1.4 Amount of £1 at various rates of inflation

	Rate of inflation (%)					
Years	*1*	*5*	*7.5*	*10*	*12*	*15*
5	1.05	1.28	1.44	1.61	1.76	2.01
10	1.10	1.62	2.06	2.59	3.11	4.05
15	1.16	2.08	2.95	4.18	5.47	8.14
20	1.22	2.65	4.24	6.73	9.60	16.37
40	1.40	7.04	18.04	45.26	93.05	267.86
50	1.64	11.47	37.19	117.39	288.99	1,083.64

within the span of a man's lifetime. Higher rates can mean that prices behave in a way which is frightening. Table 1.4 shows what happens to £1 at various rates of inflation over various periods of time.

These increases must be a very real factor in both business and personal plans. Five to ten years is a normal forward planning period for many companies. Twenty to forty years covers the length of time for which people are normally making personal provision in the form of pensions, endowment policies, and mortgages. And although we do not normally think very often of life fifty years ahead, the thought of a 15 per cent average increase causing us to have to spend over £1,000 for a purchase which today would cost £1 is positively terrifying. On this basis the 'ten bob' gallon of petrol which received so much publicity in 1974 could become the £500 gallon!

It need not be as bad as this. Certainly the inflation problem is unlikely to go away for many years, since there are major structural changes in world economies — such as the position of the under-developed countries, social expectations and entrenched patterns of behaviour — which means that the problem will remain acute for some time to come. It is also easy to become an alarmist, point to the predictions of the ecologists about expanding world populations and declining world resources, and conclude that persistent hyperinflation will be rampant for ever. This view oversimplifies the things that cause inflation, ignores the stimulus which high prices give to the production of substitutes and overlooks the ingenuity of man.

Dr Irving Friedman (1973) Economic Adviser to the President of the World Bank writes:

> Twenty years of rising prices should logically have had at least one result: recognition that the world is in a unique period of continuing universal inflation. But, after decades, this realisation is shared by few. People are well aware of the inflation in their own countries; they are not yet aware of its persistency and durability, its strength and severity, nor of its world-wide character. They need to under-

stand that prices will trend only upwards in the foreseeable future unless government policies change markedly to alter social and political behaviour as well as economics. Until this happens, some combinations of government policies and other circumstances, though not involving major change, might reduce the rate of increase in the cost of living, or even induce a short-lived levelling off of prices — but only temporarily. Continued inflation in one's country has been the only reasonable assumption for any long-run purpose.

The purpose of this chapter is to outline the parameters of the problem, and to demonstrate that it is a matter appropriate for high-level management attention. The following chapters delve deeper into the implications of inflation, and show some of the things that business can do to cope with the situation.

References

FRIEDMAN, I. S. (1973) *Inflation a World Wide Disaster*, Hamish Hamilton, p. 126.

HEATON, H. (1948) *Economic History of Europe*, Harper, p. 679.

HUSSEY, D. E. (Jan. 1974) 'How to forestall the commodity crises', *The Director*.

NATIONAL ECONOMIC DEVELOPMENT OFFICE (Sept. 1973) *Inflation and Company Accounts in Mechanical Engineering*.

2

The causes of inflation

The title of this chapter is rather ambitious, since the causes of inflation are not easily identified, and it is something of an understatement to say that there is some controversy between economists over the various theories. Even an acceptance of one of the theories does not necessarily bring an identification of the real cause. A belief that inflation is caused by the push of rising costs does not automatically lead to any solutions since the rising costs may be only a symptom: the real cause may be a wave of social unrest, a change in the tactics of organised labour, or even a new form of indirect taxation. So it is not a simple problem. There is no universal agreement over the theories, and even the theories explain only the mechanism of inflation and not necessarily its basic causal factors.

Inflation means a general rise in the level of price. Individual prices may rise even in non-inflationary conditions, and of course may be of considerable concern to individual people or particular businesses. But one swallow does not make a summer, and the isolated price increase, or the rise accompanied by equivalent price decreases elsewhere, does not make inflation. It is the upwards movement in prices in general which justifies the title. Hyperinflation is the worst stage of the disease: it is severe inflation well above the normal limits that society finds tolerable.

To Keynesian economists 'inflation is an excess of aggregate demand over supply in conditions of full employment' (Brooman, 1962, p. 227). Thus it is the state of affairs which leads to price rises, rather than the fact of the increases themselves. Similarly those economists supporting the quantity theory of money would define inflation as an increase in the supply of money, again in distinction to the price rises which this theory holds will result from an increase in the quantity of money in circulation. It is probably an abridgement of the quantity theory which leads to the common definition of inflation as too much money chasing too few goods — an expression which most of us must have used at one time or other.

For the purpose of this book I stick to the definition of inflation as I believe it is understood by businessman and housewife alike — the condition of generally rising prices mentioned above — and shall leave to the economists any quarrel over the finer shades of meaning given to the word.

The history of inflation can yield some interesting lessons which may help the consideration of causes which appears later in this chapter. Figure 2.1 is based on a fascinating study made by Phelps Brown and Hopkins (1956); The figure here has been updated and has additional information included by James Morrell.

Fig. 2.1 Seven centuries of the prices of consumables

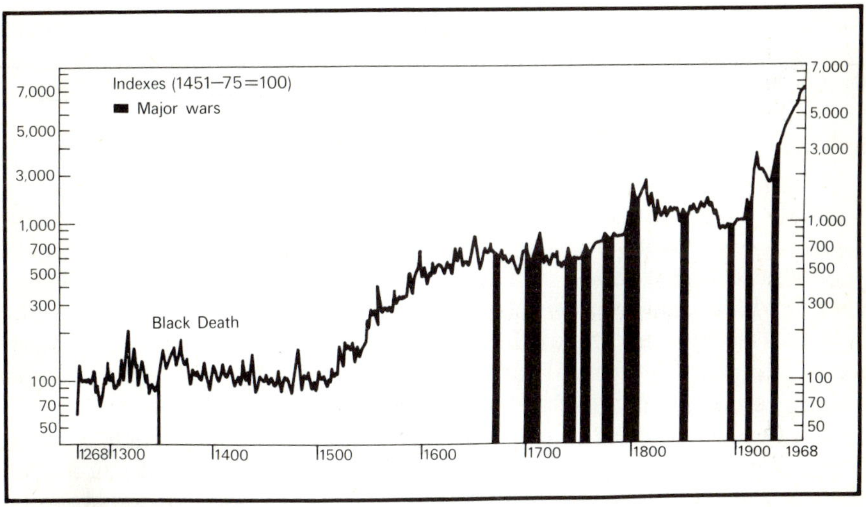

Much of the article by Phelps Brown and Hopkins is taken up with the pedigree of the data provided, for it was no simple task to collect price information relating to such a far distant period. The sources listed include, for example, Oxford College Accounts for rents paid in kind during the period 1583–1770; manorial records; Navy victualling records; hospital and college accounts; old books and newspapers. Information becomes easier to collect as the study moves towards modern times and some of the later sources are familiar. The authors also had to calculate a composite unit of consumables which took account of the changing nature of diet, domestic fuel and textiles. Potatoes, important in 1950, were unknown in 1275. The sources of this comparative data were largely household accounts of the different periods.

Many similar studies, covering much shorter periods, have been published elsewhere, and are a feature of many of the economic history books. What this particularly valuable study does is to give a unique perspective to consumer prices over a very long period. The two immediately apparent facts are that modern inflation takes a smoother course than pre-1900 inflation, and that it takes a much steeper path.

Between 1268 and 1500 prices kept to a noticeably level trend, although they fluctuated severely up or down. A century of rising prices followed (1500—1600), although again with fluctuations either side of the trend; then two centuries of relative stability, with less drastic movements from the trend. The nineteenth century reached a high point in its first quarter before it declined and entered the twentieth century at a much lower rate. From the First World War the pattern changes, and the fluctuations begin to smooth out. The depression years made a dent, but a smooth dent, in this new pattern. By the Second World War fluctuations have disappeared and the data moves only in one direction — upwards. The shape of the line alters from time to time, indicating a change in the rate of inflation, but inflation is always there. It has therefore been a factor of modern life, supported by empirical evidence for many years, that the general level of prices *never* declines.

A basically similar trend for the postwar period can be seen in statistics for most countries. Although the USA, for example, has experienced lower rates of inflation than Europe, 1949 was the last year in which there was an actual decline in prices.

Partial causes of some of the fluctuations can be read in Fig. 2.1. War is a well-known trigger of inflation, and some of the major wars have been entered on the chart. More recently, observers have noted the US jump in inflation rates brought about by the Korean and Vietnam wars. A great natural disaster, the Black Death, is also shown. This so reduced the population that wealth became more concentrated (those who died could not take their gold with them) and at the same time the available work force was greatly diminished. Much of the steep trend rise during the sixteenth century has been ascribed to the inflow of riches from the new world, particularly into Spain and Britain. For these countries, too, much of the period was taken up by wars of varying degrees of severity.

Both the world wars had the expected impact on prices — and of course the price indices cannot measure the hidden inflation such as the disappearance of some products from the market altogether, and deterioration in standards of quality. The figure suggests that many factors must have changed in the modern period to prevent the fluctuations of the past from occurring. It is interesting to speculate what some of these factors might be.

Organised labour. At the top I would put the growing power of organised labour. Whereas in previous centuries employers could enforce a wage decrease in bad times, or quite cheerfully throw people out to starve, this is not possible under modern conditions. Wage negotiations today are concerned with the size of the increase — whether measured by money, conditions, or shorter working hours — and never a decrease. At the same time there has been a change in society's attitude to employment and the treatment of people, and callous behaviour towards the individual is no longer condoned. Because the norms of society are continually changing, views of what is fair behaviour are also changing, and employers have to assume increasing obligations towards those they employ.

As a member of modern society I cannot but agree that attitudes towards employees are much better than they were in previous centuries. The moral correctness of these attitudes does not, unfortunately, stop them from contributing to the modern type of inflation.

Increased size of business. The years since the Second World War have been notable for the combining of businesses into larger units. On the one hand this has come about through nationalisation by Government of activities such as the railways and steel production. On the other, an equally active private sector has through acquisition and merger — some of it with government encouragement — produced a series of industrial empires of considerable size. Many arguments have been produced to justify this trend, including economies of scale and benefits from rationalising activities. No doubt much of the energy expended in creating big units has been beneficial, but a side effect has been to increase the bargaining strength of organised labour. It is now much easier for what might have been a local dispute to spread across the whole country, for the private and public economic effects of a strike to be much more severe, and for what would once have been an essentially local problem to become insoluble when projected into the national arena. The 1973—74 railway dispute involving ASLEF would not have become national had the old regional railways still been in existence, and the matters at issue could have been settled were it possible to deal with them on a purely regional basis. It is noticeable that rail disputes which at one time might have occurred in only one area of the country now become national, rapidly paralysing the whole of British Rail — yet rarely affecting the London Transport railway network.

The managed economy. Particularly since the Second World War, more attention has been given by all Governments to managing the economy. In the UK this has usually resulted in periods of 'go', where there has been a drive for full employment and periods of 'stop', when the inflation caused by the 'go' policies has so adversely affected the balance of payments that action has to be taken to correct this. No Government has been prepared to accept the social consequences of an unmanaged economy, where business cycles could take their natural course until severe depressions, acute unemployment and the collapse of businesses brought prices tumbling down again.

Defence expenditure. The period since the First World War has, in most countries, been characterised by a high level of defence expenditure. There has also been at least one war going on somewhere in the world, and a number of the more important countries have, sometime during this period, been engaged in some form of warfare. This has meant the diversion of a significant element of the world's resources to unproductive ends.

World development. The world has been developing at a rapid pace, in terms of trade, population, and gross national product. Demand for the world's raw materials has increased, and the role of the traditional supplying countries has begun to change as their economic and political development alters. Only the rapid development of substitutes has been a mitigating factor reducing some of the pressure on supplies. Of course commodity prices do fluctuate, and a decline in material prices is still possible — as happened in the UK in 1967 (see Table 1.3) — whereas a decline in wage and salary rates is next to impossible.

Changed world conditions have also led to a greater inter-relationship of national economies. Inflation spreads very rapidly across borders, and many of the actions taken by national governments to manage their own economies contribute to inflation in other countries. It is no consolation to point to a country which is suffering from a worse dose of the disease, for isolation is impossible and no disinfectant can destroy the contagious nature of the illness.

We have looked at the development of the inflation problem over several hundred years, and at some of the things which might help explain why postwar inflation has taken such a markedly different course. It is now appropriate to give some time to the underlying theories of the mechanism which causes inflation. These can be described as *demand-pull, cost-push* and *monetary* theories.

The demand-pull approach follows the Keynesian school and holds that inflation is caused by changes in the economy which lead to increases in demand. When an economy moves into a boom period it rapidly uses up its spare capacity, the rate of unemployment drops, unfilled vacancies increase, and output falls short of demand. Consumers want to spend their money, industries are investing in new capacity and the public sector is also spending freely — in fact it might have been an increase in public expenditure which helped the economy to reflate and so move towards its position on the upturn of the trade cycle.

This increase of demand beyond the capacity of the economy causes prices to rise, because of competition among consumers, and the economy begins to overheat. The price competition stretches back through the whole chain of production — demand for commodities and raw materials increases beyond the available supply, demand for labour increases its cost — either through the payment of higher rates to attract workers, increased overtime working, or the employment of people of lower skills and productivity. At the consumer level, people are willing to pay higher prices in order to secure what they want, and suppliers, encouraged by the higher costs they have had to pay, are not slow to see or take advantage of this opportunity.

An accompanying symptom of an inflating economy is frequent balance of payments problems, because the expansion of spending attracts imports, while rising prices are making exports less competitive in outside markets.

The remedy for this problem is deflation, that is for the Government to attempt to manage demand in such a way that the overheating is reduced and the economy once again has a measure of surplus capacity. This is usually done by the cutting of public expenditure (which plays havoc with the long-term plans of local authorities, the universities, and the health service), increased taxation to reduce consumer expenditure, and the curtailment of credit. The boom ends, the unemployment rate goes up, and the economy has entered the familiar stop phase referred to earlier in this chapter.

This theory certainly appears to explain some of the things we know about inflation. Deflation often does reduce the rate of inflation, but it has never in our postwar period caused an actual decline. It may correct the accompanying balance of payments situation, although this sometimes has to be helped along by devaluation.

Certainly the average businessman will agree that the demand/supply mix has an effect on some prices, the salary of a London secretary for example. Commodity prices react very quickly to changes in the demand and supply curves, but the prices the UK has to pay also take account of changes in the total world (or at least the free world) demand or supply. It is easy to see how the fresh fruit and vegetable market can also be very sensitive to changes in conditions, but less easy to relate the demand-pull theory to a manufacturer's normal commercial behaviour.

The chances are that if sales of his product rise, he will congratulate himself on his clever marketing, his effective advertising or his own skill in achieving his objectives: this, after all, is what he has probably been trying to do anyway. Although one or two marketing books recommend the derivation of a hypothetical demand curve, few (if any) businesses have any firm idea of their current price/demand relationships, and there can be even fewer who are able to see that the demand curve for their products has shifted, and that consumers are now willing to pay higher prices. The prices of most products are adjusted by a conscious decision (which certainly will take account of the buoyancy of the market and competitors' price levels) and not by any invisible market force.

Most businessmen will react to the higher costs they have to pay, as these begin to erode profit margins. Indeed the first effect of an expansion of demand may be to increase profits as inventories are run down, and economies of scale occur as production rises. Once the increased costs begin to work through the business, and price decisions are taken, demand-pull may be considered to be the indirect cause.

Another school of thought argues that the overheating caused by demand-pull is not the culprit at all, and that it is really the push of costs which causes the problem. Reaction to cost increases is, as discussed above, more familiar behaviour to the average businessman than judging demand changes. The cost-push theory not only looks at the increased costs of production that may come about from 'overheating', but also suggests that costs rise which have nothing to do with demand for the ultimate products.

The first example which springs to mind is the escalation in labour costs beyond the increase in productivity of that labour. It is, of course, the stronger bargaining position of organised labour which makes this possible, where the traditional supply/demand curve of labour has been drastically changed by becoming completely inelastic, with no labour available at all until the trade union's asking price is met. In theory this is big business negotiating with organised labour, with labour feeling that it is management's choice whether it recovers the increases from the consumer or through increased productivity, or pays for it from its own profits.

In theory a few groups of essential workers could demand an impossibly high wage increase, and paralyse the economy if it were refused. The UK miners' dispute in 1973–74 showed just how easily this could be done. This power will remain only so long as society is prepared to condone it.

This is not meant as an attack on the merits or otherwise of the trade union case, nor indeed is it meant as a comment on whether the unions normally act responsibly or irresponsibly. It is meant to illustrate one of the factors of modern life: that an area of cost can be increased without reference to demand, since those pressing the claim are willing to take the risk that cost changes will cause a fall in the quantity of the product purchased.

It would be incorrect and unfair to suggest that labour represents the only pull on costs which causes price inflation. Prices of commodities and raw materials can rise through factors completely unconnected with labour: world sugar prices may go up because of poor harvests resulting in a smaller supply reaching the market, or because world demand for sugar changes because Russia or China suddenly enters the field as a buyer. The domestic pull of demand in, for example, the UK has little or nothing to do with inflation of this type. The period 1973—74 was one of unprecedented increases in commodity prices, all of which undoubtedly had a deleterious effect on inflation rates. Of course it is possible to argue that the increased price of commodities is in part due to the pull of demand in the individual consuming countries, and that if this falls prices will also tumble.

It took the major oil producers of the world to demonstrate beyond all doubt that cost-push can be a valid cause of inflation. In late 1973 and early 1974 not only were supplies of oil reduced in quantity, but prices were simultaneously dramatically increased. This was partly a political weapon and partly economic, in that producers realised that by working in unison they could make consuming countries pay more. Initiative passed rapidly from the buyer to the seller. There was no way in which such massive increases in the price of energy could be absorbed by those using it, and the cost-push snake of oil prices wriggled its way through the economies of the buying nations, enmeshing in its coils virtually every form of economic activity.

Taxation, too, can cause inflation through the cost-push effect. Certainly the price of alcohol is at a far higher level than it would be were it not for the various taxes it has to pay. It is normal, and usually the intention of Government, for taxes to be passed on through the various levels of the economic system until they reach the ultimate consumer.

There is yet another point about the cost-push/demand-pull controversy. Many producers have a comparatively high breakeven point. A decrease in production caused by a reduction in demand does not necessarily mean that cost pressure will slacken — in fact the opposite can occur if 'variable' costs are not immediately variable, and they rarely are. A decline in output frequently *increases* the average cost per unit: it is very rare to find an industry so finely tuned that costs and output move together. Indeed, with a social climate which is turning increasingly against lay-offs and redundancy, the flexibility of modern business to reduce costs in the short term is very much impaired.

Some mention should be made of the third theory of the cause of inflation: the quantity theory of money. This was originally the classical theory of inflation, abandoned by many in favour of Keynes's theories, although it has recently had a revival in some quarters. This theory states that inflation is caused by an increase in the supply of money beyond the needs of the economy. When a Government produces too many banknotes these pass into the economy, stimulate spending and the price rises. Control, says this theory, can be simply exercised by reducing the supply of money — thus if banknotes are withdrawn when prices rise, demand will drop and prices will fall again.

This, of course, is a very simplified version of the theory. A more complete statement would have to take account of the velocity of circulation: the number of times each banknote is used. If, for example the velocity of circulation doubles, this will have the same effect as if the supply of banknotes doubles. It is also a fact that in a modern economy banknotes are but a part of the money supply. 'Money' is also created through the banking system, including the use of cheques and credit cards. Thus the supply of money at any one time becomes both harder to calculate and harder to control. This particular theory has been rarely used by Governments in their attempts to control inflation. The issue of banknotes has been geared to the requirements of the country, and banknotes are not withdrawn to prevent spending. Although I would agree that the completely uncontrolled issue of banknotes — provided they did in fact enter the economy through some form of spending — would be dangerous, I find it hard to accept that manipulations of a well-run policy can make any difference to inflation rates.

My own view is that inflation can be sparked off by either demand-pull, or cost-push, or a mixture of both. The practical difficulty is to diagnose which, for although the effects on business of any inflation, whatever its cause, might be the same, the cures attempted by Government will be different. Demand management, as discussed earlier, will have little effect on cost-push inflation, which needs measures aimed directly at the cost side. In these days this suggests policies which prevent cost increases from arising — in other words legal or voluntary pay and price policies, the encouragement of substitutes, and possibly some adjustments to taxation. The remedies for inflation will almost certainly have a different effect on business, depending on how Government diagnoses the illness.

Until fairly recently there appeared to be relationships between inflation and full employment. The Phillips curve, named after the man who derived it, demonstrated a constant relationship over long periods of the rate of unemployment and the annual change in wage rates. Increases were lower when unemployment rose, higher when it fell. Unfortunately, in more recent years we seem to be able to generate high inflation at the same time as unemployment increases. Thus any relationships between the two factors (and common sense suggests there must be some) have become obscured. This may be partly because of an increase in imported inflation, partly because of a change in labour's bargaining position, and partly because the base of statistics has changed. In fact we never really know how many unemployed there are, only how many are registered. Children who stay at school longer because job prospects are poor, or wives who would like to work but do not register because they know there is no chance of getting jobs, are among the areas of hidden unemployment. In addition there may be large regional differences; in the UK for example, there is often a shortage of workers in London and the south-east at a time when the level of unemployment in the country as a whole is considered unacceptable. A change may occur in any of these factors without affecting the unemployment statistics. A difference in the basic statistics also partly explains why the USA is able to find a 4 per cent unemployment rate acceptable, while in the UK this would be considered a positive disaster.

The fact that successive governments have had to juggle with problems of inflation, unacceptable levels of unemployment and balance of payments has neither aided the solution of the inflation problem, nor does it help business to forecast the extent and nature of the future inflation problem with which it will have to cope. Much of the trade cycle of the British economy has, as pointed out by Donaldson (1973, p.66) become linked to the British electoral system, with a noticeable correlation between election years and periods of economic growth.

It seems to me that two clear basic needs arise from the many problems which inflation brings to business. The first is to attempt to forecast both the future rates of inflation and Government reaction to them. The second is to assume that inflation is a cost-push and to set about ways of reducing costs. Although the viability of some of these may depend on the rate of inflation, there are numerous actions which will be valid whatever that rate may be. Thus no company should use the difficulty of forecasting as an excuse for failing to act.

The first need leads to the question, can inflation be forecast? Perhaps this should be more precisely phrased by adding the words 'with sufficient accuracy'. The answer is not simple, but one certainty can be stated: the company that studies the economy and devotes some of its resources to the problem has a greater chance of success than the company which ignores it. What is usually needed most is lead time for decisions, and this cannot be gained by the company which relies for its information on press comments on the latest retail prices index.

Few companies can afford to set up their own independent economic forecasting team, with its own model of the national economy. Most can justify the allocation of a skilled person, or persons, to the interpretation of commercially available economic forecasts, statistics and general economic data. Most countries have a number of agencies offering economic forecasting services and providing regular forecasts of the main economic factors, of which inflation is one of the most important. The best of these derive from a model of the economy. If the assumptions on which the forecasts are based are clearly defined it becomes possible to derive forecasts which are not only logically coordinated but which can also be rapidly adjusted if an assumption proves incorrect.

Few, if any, forecasting services predicted the massive oil price rises of 1973, but most were able to provide a reasonably speedy assessment of what this would do to inflation and the economy. Although plans at any one time have to be based on a particular assessment of inflation, the monitoring of those plans and many subsequent decisions should take account of revised assessments of the rate of inflation as they arise. In a situation of rapid inflation, forecasts need to be examined at least once a month: in more stable conditions the frequency may drop to once or twice in a year.

There is a need for both short and longer term inflation forecasts. Many tactical decisions require estimates of six to eighteen months ahead. Strategic decisions will require even longer: if possible of expected rates of inflation, but at least the general direction in which inflation is expected to go. An anticipated five-year period of hyper-inflation will lead the company to decisions different from those they would have made if they had expected only mild inflation, even though actual rates are not known.

Any economic forecasts are subject to considerable uncertainty, and most services make a number of forecasts which turn out to be inaccurate. However, the fact that inaccuracy is likely is something which should be dealt with in the company's planning approach, and this question is discussed at length in Chapter 5. A forecast for twelve months ahead which puts the rise in the retail prices index at 12 per cent when in fact it turns out to be 15 per cent certainly carries a relatively high percentage error. This becomes less significant if the general direction is correct — the 12 per cent assessment might well lead to better decisions than a belief that the rise would be around a 6 per cent historic trend. Subsequent revisions of the forecast, taking account of new factors, are likely to bring greater improvements in accuracy.

Thus the average business can gain considerable benefit by giving consistent attention to this forecasting problem, despite the fact that the potential error in longer-term forecasts may be relatively high, and that the best of forecasts is always at risk from an event which is virtually unpredictable — the oil situation once more.

The general rates of inflation are but one vital part of the problem facing every business. Attention must also be given to the specific factors — materials, money and labour — which make up the costs of the company's products, and the impact of these on the prices of these products. This aspect is taken up in Chapter 6. The general rate of inflation is a key factor in all this more detailed analysis. It has a direct impact on salaries and wages, and plays a part in determining consumer's spending habits.

Few companies should be satisfied with a forecast of the rate of inflation, useful though this may be, and should give equal concern to likely Government policies resulting from it. Although the exact steps which will be taken by Government may be difficult to predict, the range of options open to Government can be identified much more easily. Correct identification of what is likely can help the company in both short- and long-term decisions. Reasonable success can be gained given a good economics intelligence source and some skills at interpretation. In most of the commercially available forecasts the anticipated rate of inflation is dependent on assessments of Government policies: these are among the clearly defined assumptions stated earlier to be a feature of the best forecasting services available.

As much of modern business is multinational (and those businesses which are not should perhaps re-examine their strategy on this important issue), most businesses will be interested in comparative inflation rates in different countries. This is particularly important where there is a choice open to the company as to where it procures its future product, or where it makes an investment in new capacity. A decision taken on today's comparative costs must be checked against expectations for inflation and productivity improvement in each of the countries being considered. Today's low-cost producer may, if it suffers a very high rate of inflation, be the high-cost producer of tomorrow. Forecasting problems of domestic inflation become simple when compared with the difficulties of organising comparable forecasts for a variety of different nations.

'Productivity improvement' expresses in two words the second area of attention for the company seeking to combat inflation, the area where actions can often be implemented and which does not depend on an accuracy in forecasting inflation. A pound saved is a pound saved, whether next year's inflation runs at 6 or 10 per cent. Chapters 8, 9 and 10 deal in some depth with some of the specific ways in which attention might be given to this aspect of the problem, and discuss issues arising from purchasing, industrial relations and cost reduction approaches.

It is perhaps this area which offers the greatest hope for the solution of the inflation problem. This is the battleground on which the skill of the manager can help to hold the advance of inflation. It is unlikely that the sociological causes which currently contribute to inflation will disappear. If the costs of the factors of production continue to rise the only real solution is to ensure that less of the factors are used to produce the same amount. This is something which requires the attention of the top management team. It is a strategic issue as well as a tactical one, and on our ability to solve it hangs more, much more, than the profitability of our businesses. On this there hangs the very survival of our whole social structure.

References

BROOMAN, F. S. (1962) *Macroeconomics*, Allen and Unwin.
DONALDSON, P. (1973) *Economics of the Real World*, Penguin.
PHELPS BROWN, E. H. and HOPKINS, S. U. (Nov. 1956) 'Seven centuries of the prices of consumables compared with builders' wage rates', *Economica.*

3

The social impact of inflation

Business is concerned with developments in society for a number of reasons. The political and economic climate in which all business operates draws its strength from the community at large. As peoples' feelings and views begin to change, there is usually an effect on the laws, controls and fiscal rules to which business is subject. A change may first begin to make itself felt through pressure groups, such as conservationists, local amenity groups, the women's liberation movement and the like. These groups themselves may cause modifications to the business climate because of their power to influence, which is often the greatest strength they possess. The pressures applied by the few are often caught up in a wave of popular feeling, causing outright changes to the climate. Business may recognise these feelings and take action of its own accord, or may be forced to do certain things because the political system enacts relevant laws. Simple examples are attitudes to profits, work, equal opportunities for women, religious or racial discrimination, and profits of property companies: all these have changed in the last decade, and many are now subject to the force of law which ensures the new norms and desires of society.

So the survival of business, the way it operates, and how and where it makes its profits will depend very much on that businesss environment which is dictated by society. But business is also an integral part of society. It is a human activity, brought about by the combined actions of individual people. Because of this, many of its opportunities lie in the responsiveness of its attitude to the needs and norms of society. There are many who would argue that the responsibility of a business goes much wider than merely meeting the requirements of its shareholders, fundamental though the shareholders' interest is to the survival of any organisation.

Business employs people, and therefore should be concerned with anything which affects the values of society as a whole and the work force in particular. Changing attitudes to work, profits, and the nature of certain jobs will affect both the supply of labour (and managers) and how it is treated. Industrial relations present a current situation requiring a treatment appropriate to today, and rarely responding to the policies and actions of yesterday. (Industrial relations and inflation is the subject of Chapter 9.)

Not only does the community provide the employees of business, it also presents it with its market. Changes in the norms of behaviour, attitudes, the way people order and manage their lives and the structure of society itself all have a direct effect on the type and quantity of products an individual business may wish to offer. Sometimes these products, for example the motor car, may themselves be the agents of social change. More frequently the opposite situation applies and markets are modified by what happens within society.

Because of its interlinked role with society, business must be concerned with any major factors which are likely to contribute to changes in the values and attitudes of society. Inflation is one such factor. Levels of inflation experienced in the past have contributed to the society of today. Continual inflation, even at the average rates of the past ten years, will continue to influence the social environment. A significant increase in the rate of inflation will bring about completely new patterns of behaviour. Hyperinflation over a long period would bring such changes to our society that it would rapidly become unrecognisably different.

Some observers, for example, suggest that the social unrest and political instability of many high inflation countries, such as some of the Latin American nations, is largely brought about by the hyperinflation experienced there. In 1974, the Chancellor of the Exchequer, Denis Healey, stated in his Budget speech that 'continual severe inflation could pose a serious threat to the continuation of our present form of democracy'.

It is possible to develop a simplistic argument that inflation need have no effect on society. If prices increase by 10 per cent, and wages follow by the same amount, relative positions would appear to be maintained and the real value of incomes would be a constant. Who, then, would suffer from changes in the purely nominal value of money?

Unfortunately, this argument (which is used by many) ignores the important fact that the burden of inflation is inequitable. It has already been observed (Chapter 1) that it does not fall equally on companies or industries. It is just as unfair in its impact on the individual. Those on low incomes are hit harder than those in higher brackets, and those on low fixed incomes (pensioners) are hit hardest of all. Those with savings find the real value of their money declining, unless they are earning an after-tax rate of dividend or interest which is at least equal to the general rate of inflation. The higher the inflation, the less likely is this to be possible, and conditions of hyperinflation are likely to make spendthrifts of us all; or at least to redirect our saving habits into investment in 'things' instead of equity investments, insurance, deposits and the like. More time and energy is devoted to the protection of assets against erosion. Inflation contributes to the spread of interest in collections (for example; of antiques, pictures, gemstones and silver medals) for their capital appreciation potential rather than from the genuine collector's urge. Time and effort spent in this way, whether by business or the private individual, is generally unproductive and rarely contributes to the growth of the gross national product.

Such changed saving behaviour is more likely to be a feature of the managerial and professional components of the population; partly because such alternatives to building societies, savings banks and unit trusts require a high level of awareness and a continuous source of knowledge about prospects for the items concerned; partly because valid investments can usually only be made by people with relatively large sums of money available. An accompanying trend is therefore likely to be one of consumer spending. People begin to believe that their savings are losing value so quickly that they may as well have the full benefit of their money by spending now. Such a disenchantment can have far reaching consequences, for example:

- an upset of sources of funds fundamental to the way in which house purchases are financed;
- a severe impact on Government through the curtailment of loan funds available from the Post Office savings bank;
- a change in the way the Government exercises demand management (the more that savings can be encouraged, the less the Government needs to take out of the economy in taxation);
- an increase in the market for consumer durables and leisure activities;
- the creation of a spendthrift society relying on more Government intervention to provide basic housing and retirement benefits.

Certainly the person who saves money in the traditional way is penalised twice — by the loss of real value of his savings and through the higher rates of income tax charged on 'unearned income'.

Friedman (1973, p. 185) draws attention to a change in social habits brought about by inflation. He maintains that children now need financial help from their parents for a much longer period, beyond the point when they themselves reach adulthood and are themselves economically active. Parents frequently find themselves in the position of having to offer living space to their married children, or providing finance to help them establish homes of their own. Similarly he argues that a high rate of inflation makes it more difficult for the old to be self-supporting, and forces them to be a burden on their children. All this leads to social change in the shape of more shared dwellings and a higher financial pressure on the middle-aged economically active population, making it harder for them to provide for their own old age and ensuring that in time they too have to fall back on their own children.

Certainly some of these trends are visible in our society as it is today, and it is not difficult to imagine them escalating rapidly under conditions of continued high inflation. The impact on life style, design of homes and furnishings and on the use of leisure would be considerable. Steadily rising prices make it more difficult for the public sector to provide either for alternative housing, or for many of the other projects normally financed by central or local government. The UK already has a housing problem, as evidenced by the activities of the charity Shelter. Many will have observed the problem more closely on BBC television's experimental serial documentary 'The Family', which showed day-to-day life in an overcrowded house which was the domicile of both the parents and their married children, and this is the problem as it is now, not how it might become under the impact of continued and more severe inflation.

In all areas rising costs makes it more difficult for Government, whether central or local, to do things. We have to continue with inadequate schools built for a bygone age, a lack of modern hospitals, particularly for the mentally ill, and great difficulty in providing new civic amenities or in replacing worn out ones. Roads and railways never seem to catch up with the needs of society. Under current inflationary trends needs always run well ahead of the country's capacity to provide for them. More severe inflation will widen this gap, making it much harder for any government to meet the expectation of its citizens, and forcing the community to make do with services and facilities which already fall far short of the requirements of the age.

Friedman (1973, p. 188) observes that inflation has led to a new militancy over wage claims. 'Inflation has made "workers" and "trade unionists" out of public officials and members of professional societies. Headlines in all countries tell of policemen, garbage collectors, teachers, communications and transport workers on strike.' Severe inflation also causes other symptoms to emerge. More people feel the need to take a second job (the 'moonlighting' of the USA), with the consequent impairment of their ability to do one job well, and additional disruption of family life. More wives seek jobs in order to increase the family income, bringing consequential changes to the way they run their households and additional demands for services such as late night shopping and child minding facilities. The combined effect of working wives and a lack of housing is likely to be a reduction in the birth rate, as married couples postpone the advent of children. Modern birth control methods, which have already affected population trends, provide the tool, and family economics provide the motivation.

It would, of course, be wrong to argue that inflation is the only factor which leads to this need to supplement the family budget. Concomitant causes are the materialism of modern society and, in the case of working wives, the continuing revolution which questions the validity of the role of man as the provider and of woman as the person who minds the home and rears the children. Severe inflation is, however, likely to accelerate these trends far more than materialistic greed or the actions of Women's Lib.

With inflation causing these trends, and society reacting to the problems caused by rising prices, it is significant to note that there is strong evidence that much of the population neither understands the meaning of the term inflation nor, and this is more important, has any idea of the mechanism which causes prices to rise, Behrend *et al.* (1971) report on two surveys carried out in 1966 and 1971. Fieldwork for the first survey was carried out by Research Services, and for the second by National Opinion Polls, using samples designed to be nationally representative. In answer to the question, 'What does inflation mean to you?' 56 per cent in 1971 (69 per cent in 1966) demonstrated that they had either a low or nil understanding of the meaning of the word. In 1971 28 per cent (34 per cent in 1966) were also found to be unconscious of any connection between wage increases and price increases; a further 7 per cent (1971) had only a vague awareness of some sort of connection between the two; 18 per cent felt that higher prices lead to wage claims; less than 50 per cent considered that wage claims might result in higher prices. (See also Daniel, *The P.E.P. Survey on Inflation*, July 1975, for new research on this topic.)

Katona (1971, p. 58) noted a similar lack of association between prices and wages in surveys carried out in the USA:

> Income increases and price increases are viewed by most people as not related to each other. When survey respondents are asked why they are making more money than five or ten years ago, they commonly refer to their own efforts, to increased experience and ability, and to progress in their careers, rather than to inflation or to activities by the government and trade unions. Therefore inflation is viewed as 'bad' even by people whose income rose much more than prices advanced. Inflation detracts from the satisfaction with what is seen as the well-deserved fruits of one's labor.

Behrend poses the question that the lack of understanding of both the word and the process of inflation might well impede Government attempts to control inflation. With less than half the population believing that the moderation of wage claims would lead to less price inflation, it is not surprising that actions to control wages are not given wide support. And this, of course, does not take account of the (unknown) number of people who might see the logic of lower wage increases, but still prefer to put their own self-interest ahead of the interests of the nation.

Many businessmen might be tempted, and not entirely without just cause, to throw much of the blame for high rates of inflation on to the trade unions. Society as a whole, with its observed lack of understanding of the connection between prices and wages, is equally likely to blame business and accuse it of profiteering.

In recent years profits have been coming under increasing criticism, until in some quarters the fact that a business has made a profit tends to be increasingly viewed as an anti-social activity. (The same society also stigmatises the business which goes bankrupt because it fails to make adequate profit.) An article in *Barclays Review* (1974, p. 26) stated:

> It is also possible that the socio-political attitude to profits that has developed over the past few years may represent a significant threat. The underlying doctrine has the positive element of firms' social responsibility and the negative one that profits are disreputable. The practical implications are manifest both in the prices and incomes policies and in the public statements and actions of industry and organised labour. In more extreme circles phrases like 'while capitalism survives' are beginning to be heard. Certainly if the doctrine continues to develop along the present lines the effect on the private sector will be debilitating and eventually make it an anachronism. Militant elements in labour organisations are apparently out to accelerate this process.

The social responsibility doctrine is with us now, as is a strong body of opinion which castigates profits as immoral. In an inflationary situation society can speedily be persuaded that the problem is entirely due to the selfish behaviour of business. Profits, and therefore capitalism, are attacked, and those already motivated through political belief to the destruction of free enterprise find their arms full of readymade ammunition.

It is my belief that a continued high inflation rate poses a very real threat to the survival of business as we know it today. This, at least as much as any other reason, provides justification for management interest in inflation, and for companies to do all in their power to curb the rate. Put simply, it is survival. The penalty for failure is nationalisation or worker control on a very wide scale. Social attitudes do not have to move very far left of where they are today in order to bring this about.

Inflation also exacerbates feelings of social injustice, of which a criticism of profits may be one manifestation. With few groups of people themselves willing to accept less, there is nevertheless a feeling that certain sections of the community should have more. Once again there has to be a scapegoat, and this time it is often the captains of industry. High inflation tends to exaggerate social class divisions, and to produce feelings of 'them and us'.

The high salary earner is penalised by the tax system as well as inflation. Although he may not have to change his eating habits — which can happen with the pensioner or low-paid worker — the purchasing power of his income is reduced. Tax allowances are changed infrequently, and have no automatic adjustment to take account of inflation. The bands at which higher rates of tax apply also change but rarely. The £10,000-a-year man of today may pay the same monetary tax as the £10,000-a-year man of yesterday, but the real value of his net income is much less. The same effect can be seen in the way that tax returns have to be sent by business to the authorities to show travelling and entertainment expenses of employees over a certain income. Once this requirement embraced only middle management and upwards. Now, because of inflation, it covers secretaries, clerical workers and many others who certainly fell outside the intention of the original regulations. Changes are planned but are years behind their time.

Continued high inflation is also likely to have another deleterious effect on sociopolitical opinion, although some managers might view this as an advantage. It is the lessening of interest in ecology and the preservation of the environment. In the few years immediately before the 1973 inflation bombshell, the conservationists had done a great deal to awaken public concern about pollution, the failure of modern society to recycle raw materials, and the general controversy over the natural limits to world growth, through overpopulation and the gradual exhaustion of raw materials. The arguments now familiar, are developed, for example in Ward and Dubos (1972) and Meadows *et al.* (1972).

Solutions to many of the problems posed by the conservationists are technically possible and generally costly, yet there was much progress towards implementing many of them, to the benefit of both present and future generations. High inflation focuses attention on the problems of today at the expense of tomorrow. Political success lies in reducing inflation rates now rather than in protecting the world against pollution and possible economic impairment in the future. Politicians become less interested in conservation, and relax standards which have already been established.

The immediate need to keep the economic ship afloat leads to, for example, an urgent expansion of nuclear power stations, despite the fact that many safety questions remain unanswered, and there is still no safe solution of the problem of the disposal of radioactive wastes. The environmental lobby holding up the building of a pipeline to bring Alaskan oil to the USA meets an even more powerful lobby seeking a domestic oil supply at all costs. Arguments against the extraction of oil from shale, which may literally mean moving mountains, are defeated by the same problem of urgent need, and areas of great natural beauty become sacrifices on the altar of the god of rising costs. The more difficult the supply position, the more violent the rise in prices, the more likely are economic decisions to be based on short-term 'stop the rise' criteria, rather than on long-term decisions in the best interest of mankind.

On top of this, inflation makes it harder for either Government or industry to meet the capital cost of environmental improvement. The sums involved in meeting the need, for example, for pollution control make it less and less attractive for business to make voluntary improvements, particularly if it is suffering from inflation-induced cash flow problems and, if the effect of such an expenditure is to increase prices still further, society will tend to be less stringent in its demands for less pollution.

So far attention has been given to a number of social trends which are likely to develop to a greater or less extent according to the rate at which inflation increases. Most of these are a more pronounced manifestation of trends already present in society. Some threaten the profits of business, others change the marketing opportunities open to business, providing new situations which can be profitably exploited to satisfy consumer needs.

Little has been said about the direct impact of inflation on consumer purchase behaviour. Studies of this problem have been made regularly in the USA over a period of years, and are reported by Katona (1971). In addition to the relationship of earnings to inflation mentioned earlier, he found that inflation was regarded as an evil by the vast majority of Americans. He reports on a retardation of consumer demand brought about by inflation which appears

> to contradict the widely held notion that consumers who expect prices to go up try to beat inflation by buying in advance and in excess of their needs. This theory, although confirmed in periods of hyperinflation in some foreign countries, is not in line with the attitudes and behaviour of American consumers.

Most consumers in fact economise or postpone purchasing decisions as a protection against price increases, rather than purchasing additional supplies in anticipation of increases.

It is probable that similar behaviour occurs in the UK. Additional purchases would appear to be brought about more easily by rumours of shortages, rather than expected price rises. During the three-day-week of early 1974 it was newspaper reports about expected supply problems which swept the supermarket shelves clean of toilet rolls and detergents, not the fact that inflation was at that time running at an annual rate of 13 per cent, and all the signs were that it would rise still further. Pre-Budget spending in anticipation of increases in taxation does take place, but is not a factor of overriding importance and is the prerogative of the few rather than a universal pattern of behaviour.

Factors acting against attempts to lay in stocks are the lack of storage space in many homes, the perishable nature of many food products, and the fact that many consumers lack the cash resources needed to take this sort of action. Whether the pattern would change under conditions of acute hyperinflation is another matter. Living with an inflation rate of 20 per cent or more per year might be expected to bring out new types of behaviour which do not apply when the rate is 10 per cent or less. In the worst recorded case in the Germany of the 1920s wages ended up being paid every hour, were taken away in sacks and wheelbarrows and spent before they could lose value, for prices too increased several times a day. It is to be hoped that this sort of chaos will never occur again, for in such circumstances money no longer fulfils its function as a store of value and goods are preferred instead.

Inflation can affect the size of markets. If everything moved equally markets would stay the same in real terms, although their monetary value would alter. We have already seen that inflation rarely strikes with equity and that there is a tendency for consumers to try to cut expenditure as prices rise. The impact on any one market will depend on how essential the goods are to the consumer and whether there are effective substitutes. The real value of the general food market in broad terms is less likely to be affected than the real market for petrol or motor cars, and within the general food market the luxuries and fringe products may be expected to decline much sooner than the staples. Only a general principle can be defined: each particular market must be studied separately. The message is, of course, that these studies should be made by the forward-looking business, for failure to do so can lead to many unpleasant surprises.

Conclusions will be affected by whether the economy is facing inflation and growth, or 'stagflation' — the inflating but stagnant economy. In the first situation the impact of price increases on markets may be softened by the general availability of an expanding consumers' disposable income, both in terms of earnings and readily available credit. In times of stagflation not only do prices rise, but the cash and credit in the hands of consumers stays static or declines, leaving many markets (for example most consumer durables) to suffer a double blow.

It would be naïve to pretend that changes in sociopolitical and socioeconomic behaviour are caused by a single factor. The engines that turn the mechanisms of change are usually very complex. Each factor interacts with many others, sometimes re-inforcing, sometimes obstructing, so that the final causes of social change are a compound that often defies identification. Yet even with this rider, it is apparent that few of the social results of inflation are to the benefit of business, and some produce a threat to both our present democracy and the future of private enterprise. The situation is not black-and-white, but many of the shades of grey can be distinguished from each other and seem to be of the darker hues.

The individual business should be concerned by the trends, and should allocate some of its resources to their study, both in terms of conventional marketing research methods, and the use of some of the modern approaches to futures forecasting. Failure to do this can at the best result in lost profits and unnoticed opportunities; at worst it can be a corporate disaster.

References

BEHREND, H., DAVIES, J., PATERSON, E. and ROSE, E. (1971) 'What does the word inflation mean to you?' and 'What is the connexion between wages claims and prices?', *Industrial Relations Journal*, 2, no. 3; findings from two National Sample Surveys in 1966 and 1971.

FRIEDMAN, I. S. (1973) *Inflation a World-Wide Disaster*, Hamish Hamilton.

KATONA, G. (1971) 'Inflation: impact on consumer attitudes and behaviour', in *Containing Inflation in the 1970s*, M. E. Levy (ed.), The Conference Board, New York.

BARCLAYS BANK (1974) 'Whither private sector?', *Barclays Review*, 49, no. 2, May.

MEADOWS, D. H., MEADOWS, D. L., RANDERS, J. and BEHRENS, W. W. (1972) *The Limits to Growth*, London, Earth Island Ltd.

WARD, B. and DUBOS, R. (1972) *Only One Earth*, Penguin.

4

The international impact

Inflation is a worldwide problem, and in these days of international interdependence it is almost impossible for any one country to escape the ravages of the disease. But while no nations may be completely untouched, the rate of inflation can and does vary between countries, being affected by the policies of national governments, the structure of the economy and the reactions of its society.

It is all too easy to see inflation in its domestic context, and to forget the wider implications that occur when rates of inflation are uneven between countries. Government policies are primarily directed to the reactions of the electorate, and wage earners: housewives are concerned with the prices they have to pay for the goods and services they require, compared with the income from which to make these purchases; in business, most managers will be considering the current problems of their organisations. Few politicians, housewives or managers have many thoughts to spare to ponder on whether their counterparts in America, Germany, France or Nigeria face worse, equal, or lesser difficulties.

From time to time we do obtain a feeling of dubious satisfaction when we read in the newspapers that things are bad in other places. This is usually a misery loves company sort of response, a feeling that if others are also suffering from high inflation perhaps our policies and actions are not so bad after all. Such considerations are usually satisfied when we learn that inflation in those other countries is also high. We rarely dig deeper to study how high it is in relation to our own high rate.

There is a fundamental economic reason why we should be concerned with comparative inflation rates, and this is that our international competitive position may be threatened if we have a higher rate of inflation than anyone else.

Pen (1958, p. 98) draws attention to the factors which cause a country to have exports.

We may again state that exports depend on two factors. The first is the overall foreign demand. This is a quantity on which a country cannot exert much influence, although nowadays attempts are being made to control the international economic situation by joint consultation. If the size of the total foreign market is given, the question is what share a country will have in these total sales. This depends on the competitive position which that country occupies in respect of other countries, which is composed of three elements: the quality of the product (in relation to what other countries have to offer), the price level of exports in relation to the prices asked by the other countries, and the rate of exchange.

Two of the three factors — price and rate of exchange — can be directly influenced by inflation. The remaining factor, the quality of the product can be affected by inflation over time, except when the country is in a rare monopoly situation, or is able to form a cartel with other producers (such as the OPEC initiative over oil). Higher prices may encourage the development of production elsewhere, the use of substitutes, or a reduction in demand, which in turn may influence the economies of scale of the producer country.

To the quality of the product should be added another form of quality: the reliability of delivery promises and (in many cases) continuation of after sales services. A country suffering from hyperinflation and a higher than average level of labour disputes, with the resultant loss of production due to strikes, go-slows, overtime bans or the refusal to implement changes which will improve productivity, stands a very good chance of slipping many rungs down the competitive ladder.

A change in a country's competitive position affects more than exports. It is likely also to encourage imports, as foreign goods become more attractive. The balance of visible trade is thus adversely affected by falling exports and rising imports. Invisibles can be similarly stricken — tourist receipts may fall as the country becomes too expensive compared with alternative places for holidays; other services may suffer in a similar manner.

The third component of balance of payments, capital movements, may also change. Foreign inflows of money for investment may cease as the opportunities for profit reduce, and outflows of capital increase for the same reason.

The Hudson Institute Europe (1974, p. 29) draws attention to this process as it affects the United Kingdom.

> Inflation is a very important determinant of how a country competes internationally. Inflation is usually discussed in terms of how much it cuts into or even eliminates real wage increases. It must be emphasised that a country with high inflation rates must not only worry about how this directly affects the domestic economy but also how

> it affects the nation's competitive situation internationally. Regardless of the identifiable causes of inflation — be they higher import prices, higher wage costs, or excess demand conditions, or a combination of all — to suffer from a higher rate of inflation than one's competitors means disadvantage in the international market place.

Table 4.1 Consumer price (average annual increase in percentages)

	1962–66	*1966–69*	*1969–73*
USA	1.4	3.8	4.9
Japan	6.2	4.9	7.6
West Germany	2.9	2.4	5.4
France	3.9	4.1	6.1
UK	3.6	4.1	8.0
Italy	5.6	2.4	6.3

Source: OECD.

The report shows from Table 4.1 how Britain is losing the competitive advantage which low inflation rates may once have given it over other countries.

> Looking at the prospects for Britain's competitiveness over the remaining years of the decade, the forecast is rather gloomy. A country which has an important dependence upon labour — intensive industry cannot live for long with small productivity increases and rapidly increasing labour costs. Productivity must rise sharply by means of increases in technology, labour, performance, or both. For Britain to try to keep wage increases to a minimum may be a logical endeavour but this will certainly be very difficult to achieve in the years to come, especially in view of the overall conditions of relative decline in living standards. A country with 84 per cent of its exports made up of manufactured products cannot afford an inefficient secondary sector. But this is what Britain has today. To maintain or regain competitiveness, cost advantages, reliability and innovation are needed. Britain today is falling behind in all three respects.

Inflation may have a cumulative adverse effect on an established country's competitive position. It can quickly become disastrous for the underdeveloped country. The round of inflationary increases which followed the raising of oil prices in late 1973 and subsequently, has had a devastating effect on the economies of the poorer countries. A leader in the *Daily Telegraph* (1974) states:

> Extortionate oil prices have proved an even greater disaster for the poor countries of the world than for the wealthy, as is shown in a shattering report by the World Bank. On one side a notch in the belt over a well-filled stomach, a shock to a robust system, a challenge to

> powerful muscles. On the other, those just emerging from debilitating poverty see their painfully laid plans for progress suddenly wrecked. This is a tragedy on a vast scale. 800 million people who would otherwise have achieved an annual growth rate of 6 per cent may see none of that. The developing countries are not only hit by the fourfold increase in the price of the oil on which their new communications, industries and other economic activities have come to depend. Equally serious are the repercussions of the slump and increased inflation in the industrialised countries. In present circumstances it seems unlikely that the flow of aid and investment to the developing countries can be maintained at the present level, let alone increased.

Severe world hyperinflation punishes the poor country more than the rich, in much the same way as within a country the poorest members of society find the effects hardest to bear. In the longer term, the inability of poor countries to finance their development, to bring in the necessary machinery, fuel and fertilisers, can lead to a fall in the supply of certain basic commodities, adding another force to the inflationary spiral. Few poor countries have oil or other mineral resources which yield sufficient in exports to finance the additional cost of imports, and make up for the loss of capital flows in aid or investment.

So far much of the discussion has concentrated on the simple assumption that economic growth or decline comes about because of the comparative price of products, as influenced by the rates of inflation of different countries. This is only part of the story, and the quotation from Pen above draws attention to another influencing factor, the relative rates of exchange between currencies. If these remain constant, relative inflation rates will be the main determinant of changes in the prices of exports and imports. If they do not remain constant, the additional rise in prices through inflation may be intensified by a revaluation of currency, or (in the short term) reduced by a devaluation.

Rates of exchange are, of course, strongly influenced by the balance of payments situation which, as has been stated, may in turn be affected by changes in a country's competitive position. To a very large degree the rate of exchange of a nation's currency may be a political decision, and government action in support of its currency may prevent a devaluation for relatively long periods. If the underlying competitive trend is adverse, the effect on the balance of payments may be expected to worsen progressively, and ultimately devaluation will result.

The Hudson Institute Europe (1974, p. 30), refers to the effect that defence of the pound in the face of a worsening competitive position has had on the British economy.

> Traditionally, the publication of adverse trade figures sent a shudder

through the exchange markets and prompted an outflow of funds from London, forcing the authorities (under a regime of fixed rates) into considerable and costly exchange support of the pound. In the 1950's and early 1960's devaluation of the pound, a key currency, was unthinkable. Defence of the prestige of sterling and of the reputation of the cuts was responsible for much of the unhappy stop-go sign of postwar economic policy.

The change to the floating pound in 1973 ended the era of fixed rates, and has meant that some of the increases in export prices have been offset through the exchange rates of the foreign buyer. There is a penalty to this, too, for imports will cost more because of the devaluation effect which, for a country like the UK dependent on a high level of imported food and raw materials, tends to feed the fires of inflation, helping to accelerate the long-term competitive decline.

When business was mainly conducted by national rather than international companies investment would probably be made in production for the domestic market, possibly sheltering behind the customs tariff, even though the same goods might be capable of being produced more cheaply in another country. Much of the impetus of such investment decisions would have been as much because of ignorance of the opportunities elsewhere as because of more noble reasons such as patriotism. If present differential production costs are unknown, it is highly unlikely that any effort could be made to forecast the future trends of these differentials.

Since the Second World War, and particularly in the last ten to twenty years, the rules of the game have changed. Much more of business strategy is thought out across a world front, by international companies which, because of the growth of trading areas such as the EEC, are able to think not only of the best competitive area for their investment, but also in terms of rationalisation of existing national plants, and the concentration of investment into larger units serving many countries, rather than the single-country plants that made the historic pattern. These companies are well aware of the costs and trends in countries throughout the world, and will generally make their decisions with an awareness of the facts.

This does not necessarily mean that existing plants are immediately closed down. In the first instance it could be that major expansion or diversification schemes are diverted to other countries. Where the question of ceasing production does occur, it may be influenced by Government policies or the general social climate, and will be taken in the light of not only the present comparative costs between countries, but also of the expected trends of these.

Some of the gloomier forecasts of the UK. such as that of the Hudson Institute mentioned earlier, suggest that the UK's competitive position has worsened since the Second World War, and is likely to continue to worsen in the future. Any multinational companies placing credibility in this forecast cannot fail to be influenced by it in their strategic decisions affecting the UK.

It could be argued that action to withhold investment, or switch it to another country, is unpatriotic, and against the interests of society. This is one point of view, which will undoubtedly influence the thinking of some managers. Against that is the fact that in an increasingly competitive international marketing forum, it may be suicidal for a country deliberately to keep itself at a cost disadvantage when compared with other producers in the market place. Ultimately this too could result in closure of domestic plants, this time through bankruptcy and with a loss of both profit and market share.

These are generalisations, and what actually happens will be a compound of many factors, not least of which is management skill and competence. What does emerge is a strong feeling that the effects of a decline in a nation's competitive ability is likely now and in the future to have a much greater adverse effect on economic growth than has been the case in the past. The 'stagflation' syndrome comes into being: although stagnation may be an optimistic view and decline just as likely.

It would be foolish to suggest that comparative rates of inflation are the sole determinants of the rate of growth of different countries. The importance of reliability and industrial peace has already been mentioned. In addition it is possible to add many other factors, such as technology, the stage of economic growth the country has reached, the manpower and other resources of the country, the social and taxation policies of government, the quality and ability of managers and workers, and the age and efficiency of the plant and machinery used in that country. Japan, for example, for many years has had both a high inflation rate and a high growth rate, and there are many valid reasons for this. Nevertheless, the exception does not prove the rule, and inflation remains a very important factor in determining a nation's future position in the world economy.

The competitive standing of many countries has changed over the last two decades, and is continuing to change. A number of forecasts have been published from time to time by various bodies, most showing the United Kingdom sliding many places lower in the economic growth tables. Forecasts are forecasts, and by no means certainties, but the pattern suggested should be a matter of concern to every manager.

Business International (1972, pp. 16, 55) makes the predictions given in Table 4.2, showing how the position of the UK is expected to decline relative to certain other countries.

If these countries are ranked by per capita GNP, a number of them change position. This is shown in Table 4.3.

The Hudson Institute (1974, p. 8) has this to say about the economic performance of the United Kingdom:

Table 4.2 Economic growth – selected countries

	Population (millions)		*GNP (1968 $billion)*		*Per capita GNP (1968 $)*	
	1968	*1980*	*1968*	*1980*	*1968*	*1980*
Japan	101.1	113.0	141.9	445.3	1,404	3,941
Australia	12.0	14.6	26.7	52.1	2,225	3,568
New Zealand	2.7	3.7	4.8	8.6	1,778	2,324
France	50.0	54.8	126.6	227.4	2,532	4,150
Germany	60.2	64.0	132.2	237.4	2,196	3,709
Italy	52.8	57.8	74.8	142.2	1,417	2,460
Netherlands	12.7	14.8	25.2	45.3	1,984	3,060
Switzerland	6.1	6.7	17.2	26.0	2,820	3,881
UK	55.3	59.0	102.1	154.3	1,846	2,615
Spain	32.4	35.8	25.2	47.9	778	1,338

Source: Business International.

Of all the industrialised and developed economies, Britain has always had one of the lowest growth rates. Between 1949 and 1963 Britain's annual growth was at the rate of 2.6 per cent. This compares with 4.6 per cent in France, 7.8 per cent in Germany and 5.8 per cent in Italy. Over the last eighteen years it has averaged 2.8 per cent, less than half the average growth of the French, the Italians and the Spaniards, two-thirds that of the Dutch, and four-fifths that of the US. On a ten-year average since 1963, the result is the same. And most recently (1970), there has been no improvement apart from an exceptional year in 1973 when Britain's GNP grew by 5.4 per cent following a reflationary policy of the government. In fact, since

Table 4.3 Ten countries ranked by per capita GNP

Rank	*1968*	*1980*
1	Switzerland	France
2	France	Japan
3	Australia	Switzerland
4	Germany	Germany
5	Netherlands	Australia
6	UK	Netherlands
7	New Zealand	UK
8	Italy	Italy
9	Japan	New Zealand
10	Spain	Spain

> 1955, the GNP has grown by more than 4 per cent on only four occasions: in 1959, 1963, 1964 and 1973. Each of those years was ordinarily followed by deterioration in the balance of payments, deflationary measures to compensate this, and a period of further low growth.

The same report (p. 15) suggests a considerable change in the future economic position of the UK compared with its neighbours.

> Whichever way it is calculated, the size of the British economy still shows the same trend — a constant decline in relation to its neighbours. On current prices and exchange. Britain was about the same size as the German economy in 1960 but only 60 per cent their size in 1972. A figure of 50 per cent must be projected for 1980. In comparison with France. Britain will drop from 120 per cent of the size of the French economy in 1960 to a projected two-thirds of its size in 1980. . . .
>
> We will take the figures given by the OECD for 1972 Ranking GDP per capita expressed in US dollars at current prices and exchange rates, we find that Britain's per capita GDP comes eleventh out of eighteen. Britain already is behind all of its major European neighbours except Italy. Projecting six years into the future, to 1980. Britain becomes thirteenth, about the same as Italy and followed only by Greece, Ireland, Spain and Portugal among the OECD's member states.

Anyone is entitled to believe or disbelieve the forecasts, and no doubt others will be made before we reach 1980. It is less easy to deny the past, and even those who reject the forecasts utterly and completely, must admit that international positions have changed. If only a fraction of this change is attributable to inflation, it is revealed as a threat to the future. If it causes more than a fraction it should be seen as a serious enemy to the economy.

Before leaving the international scene it is interesting to study the example of Brazil. Indexation has been suggested as a remedy for inflation in various spheres of the British economy, and will occur in this book in the chapters dealing with industrial relations and inflation accounting. In Brazil we have the example of a country which has used indexation for many years as a means of coming to terms with inflation.

B. de Oliveira Campos (1974) (a former Brazilian Minister of Finance) refers to the preconditions of the Brazilian experience.

> But if the Brazilians have not the merit of inventing indexation, they discovered the need for cohabitation with inflation and acted rather boldly to generalise its application, in an effort to convert sin into virtue. *Historical, structural and political* reasons, which may not be present elsewhere, combined to render the experiment both possible

and reasonably successful. *Historically*, there was a tradition of chronic inflation. In the immediate postwar period inflation hovered around 11 per cent per year, rising to 17 per cent between 1948 and 1958, galloping into a pace of over 30 per cent between 1959 and 1963 escalating to more than 80 per cent in 1963 and exploding into a rate of over 100 per cent in the first quarter of 1964. *Structurally*, the existence of a dualistic economy with surplus labour, in either overt or disguised unemployment, particularly in the north-east, facilitated the implantation of wage restraints. Also the trade unions did not trace their creation to social battles in the market place, but originated rather from paternalistic prodding by the Government, thus lacking some of the political combativeness and revindicatory vigour of trade union movements elsewhere. *Politically*, the near chaos into which the country was plunged in 1963 and early 1964 created a yearning for social discipline, and rendered acceptable some temporary constraints on two of the traditional revindicatory coalitions — Congress and the trade unions — which, indispensable as they are in modern societies, do tend either to inflate the Government spending budget or to push wages beyond the limits that can be accommodated by productivity increases, or yielded by a reasonable manipulation of income policies.

The Brazilian solution, as described in the above report, was a mixture of statutory controls and indexation. There was general indexation of all forms of saving and loans. This move helped to correct the growing loss of confidence in money as a store of value, and the consequent destruction of the savings motive or the channelling of savings into undesirable directions, such as the hoarding of foreign currency. The result was an improvement in the financial market and the general availability of loan funds for all purposes.

Wage control was given legal backing and prevented wage claims at intervals of less than twelve months. Allowable increases were based on a complex formula which took account of real wage movements, a Government calculated productivity increase, and half of the rate of inflation expected during the next twelve months. Wage control was supported by a social programme to provide improved living and educational conditions. The effect of wage control has been to reduce the wage-push element in inflation, and to prevent the disruption of the wage structure by powerful labour groups.

Indexation was carried through to taxation, which enforced the use of inflation accounting, since taxes, profits and depreciation allowances are computed on capital assets which are revalued according to an official index. Tax exemption thresholds are also indexed, avoiding the situation which occurs in the UK where the real value of exemptions and concessions is eroded every year. Foreign exchange rates are periodically devalued in small steps and at irregular intervals on an index basis, which takes account of the internal wholesale price index and the estimated rate of inflation incurred by the main trading partners.

The result of the indexation measures was a fall in the rates of inflation, accompanied by a high rate of economic growth. From the high rates quoted earlier in the chapter, inflation fell 20 per cent to an annual 25 per cent between 1967 and 1969 and even further to between 15 per cent and 20 per cent in 1972 and 1973.

> The real success however lies not so much in the deceleration of inflation — for it remains at levels still considered unacceptable in Western societies — but in reconciling it with a very high rate of growth — over 10.3 per cent in real terms for the last five years and a hefty 11.4 per cent in 1973. The per capita income in the last five years increased by some 40 per cent in real terms (Campos, 1974).

Compare this with the recent performance in the UK, where inflation rates of around 20 per cent have been accompanied by nil or minute rates of economic growth: the three-day week may be the popular reason for the poor performance of 1974, but this does not make the lack of economic growth any less a fact.

Brazil's remedy may not be capable of direct transplant to any other country. Nevertheless, some of the actions taken must influence thinking on methods of inflation control throughout the world. The emphasis of the Brazilian method is on control, rather than cure. It does not remove inflation, but it can help to reduce its impact and to make it bearable.

Indexation will increasingly become an inflation control tool in the United Kingdom. Brittain (1974) stated: 'We have reached a point where indexation is almost the only economic issue that matters.'

Primarily, the international aspects of inflation are matters of Government policy, and the average businessman can do little to influence the different rates. He must be very much concerned with the issues, partly because they affect economic performance of the country within which he operates, and partly because his decisions must increasingly be taken in an international framework. He can no longer afford to be ignorant of the international scene, nor can he shelter behind the bulwarks of his geographical barriers. If he does not take advantage of the new set of circumstances which may emerge, his competitors will, and he will find himself increasingly at a disadvantage.

In the international aspects, as with every other facet of inflation, the rewards will go to those who act to benefit from new patterns of opportunity, or react the quickest to new sets of adverse circumstances.

Business has always needed planning and decision-making skills of a high order. The international implications of inflation calls for even more effort and skill to be applied in these areas. The penalty can be severe for those who fail to appreciate this point.

References

BRITTAIN, S. (1974) 'Indexation — now almost the only issue', *Financial Times*, 18 April.

BUSINESS INTERNATIONAL (1972) *Managing the Multi-Nationals Preparing for Tomorrow*, Allen and Unwin.

CAMPOS, R. DE OLIVIERA (1974) *Inflation in Brazil. the principles of monetary correction.* The Chairman's Lectures, The Stock Exchange, London, 19 November.

DAILY TELEGRAPH (1974) 'Poor countries tragedy', 23 September.

HUDSON INSTITUTE EUROPE (1974) *The United Kingdom in 1980*, Associated Business Programmes Ltd.

PEN, J. (1958) *Modern Economics*, Pelican (1965 translation).

5

Towards a solution – corporate planning

The first chapters of this book have dwelt on problems and issues without presenting any clear solutions. Certain trends and situations which arise from inflation have been described, but so far only modest guidance has been given to the practical manager seeking to control his business and to defend it against the ravages of inflation. Few enemies can be defeated unless they are understood, and the emphasis on issues and their effects is the first step to knowing and comprehending the enemy, inflation, so that its attacks may be thwarted.

Although some of the inflation issues have been left for later discussion, most of the remaining chapters of this book will focus on solutions. Fortunately there are many positive steps which business can take, and although none of them offers a complete answer in itself, collectively they can do much to help. Each makes a contribution to solving the problem, and the application of the concepts to the individual organisation should lead to the development of new ideas. Certainly few businesses will find a solution unless they are prepared to think about the problem and the various ways it might be tackled.

Perhaps the most obvious need any organisation can have is to practise an approach to management which ensures that environmental factors are taken into consideration during the decision-making process. This involves identifying factors which may have an impact on the company, forecasting how they will develop, and monitoring to see whether the forecasts are correct. Such a scrutiny enables the company to evaluate the threats and opportunities which arise from the environment and to ensure that strategies take due account of them. By 'environment' is meant all those circumstances external to the business which impinge on its operations. A comprehensive study would include social, political, demographic, technological, legal and economic factors, and as, has been demonstrated, inflation has implications which may affect a number of these areas.

Of course it is possible for businesses to be aware of what is going on in the world around them without setting up any special and formal methods to this end. In some situations newspapers, journals and the functional interests of managers (such as expecting the Company Secretary to be aware of impending changes to the Companies' Act) are sufficient. Informal methods have the disadvantage that they can result in different interpretations of the same event in different parts of the company, they rarely attempt both to forecast and to monitor the accuracy of forecasts, and they have a habit of missing out key items just at the time they are most required.

It is possible to overcome some of these defects by formalising the interpretation of this sort of business intelligence within the organisation. Even better is to go one step further and practice corporate planning: this is the only process of management I know of which really attempts to see that these factors are properly considered when decisions are made. It is the one approach which continually strives to relate the company to its environment.

Companies which practise corporate planning in an effective and meaningful manner are more likely to be able to put themselves in a position to cope with changes in external factors. This is why corporate planning should be one of the first weapons selected for the fight against inflation.

Corporate planning is more than a management technique. It is a way of running a company which is in tune with the thinking of the modern manager. It is more than 'planning', which few would deny is a key part of every manager's task, and embraces setting objectives, organising, motivating, and controlling. These words will be familiar to all who have read any of the leading works on management, for they describe elements of the management task identified by writers from Fayol to Drucker. Table 5.1 sets out the elements as perceived by a number of these writers and although there are some differences there are many common thoughts. Corporate planning can be shown to cover all of them. This leads to the question of why the term 'corporate planning' was ever coined, instead of 'corporate management' which is now finding favour within local government in the UK. There is, of course, much more to management than practising corporate planning, but at the same time it does represent a good cross-section of the complete management task.

Despite the defectiveness of its title, corporate planning does, as its name suggests, involve the preparation of plans. It is an integrated planning process, involving both the long and the short term and having links with the budgetary control system. In an organised and formal way it attempts to make plans which will carry the company forward to some future date, and (as has been said) does this in full consideration of events and trends in the business environment.

Table 5.1 Elements of management task functions or process distinguished by certain writers

Name	*Reference*	*Elements identified*
P. Drucker	*Practice of Management*, Pan, 1969, pp. 409—12.	Set objectives, organise, motivate and communicate, measure, develop people.
H. Fayol	*General and Industrial Management*, trans. C. Storrs, Pitman, 1969, pp. 3, 5—6.	Planning, organisation, command, coordination, control.
E. L. F. Brech	*Organisation*, Longman, 1966, p. 14.	Plan, motivate and coordinate, control.
W. H. Newman	*Administrative Action: The Techniques of Organisation and Management*, Prentice Hall, 1963.	Planning, organising, assembling resources, supervising, controlling.
L. F. Urwick	*The Pattern of Management*, University of Minneapolis Press, 1956, p. 52.	Forecast, plan, organise, direct, coordinate, control, communicate.
G. F. Milward	*An Approach to Management*, Macdonald and Evans, 1946, pp. 35—6.	Forecasting, planning and programming, organisation, command, coordinate, control.
H. Koonz	*Towards a Unified Theory of Management*, McGraw-Hill, 1964, pp. 248—9.	Planning, organising, staffing, direction, control.

(*Note:* The reader is referred to R. N. Antony, *Planning and Control Systems: a framework for analysis*, Harvard University Press, 1965, for a more detailed treatment of this subject.)

The length of time for which plans will be prepared may vary. There is no single answer which suits all companies, though five appear to have a strong and almost mystical appeal to many. Certainly the plan should be long enough to cover the lead time of decisions about to be taken, so that the expected outcome can be considered. It is little use preparing a three-year plan if the largest decision it refers to, perhaps a major new plant, can only come on stream in the fourth year. It is also helpful if the plans can envelop normal business events for the company concerned, such as any cyclical trends, or the normal lead time for the development of a new product. These can be no more than guides, and if taken to extremes could result in a plan which covered 120 years for forestry companies planting oak trees.

Too long a period tends to lead to a feeling of remoteness, and although it is often useful to take an outline strategic look beyond the normal planning period, it is hard to get serious management involvement in things which appear to outlive their own expected span of influence. As it is, the average five-year plan usually covers a period that will see many of the managers who contributed to it in different jobs, and many of them may leave the company during its course. The important thing is to push thinking forward past the frontiers of the annual budget so that management in general is required to consider the wider implications of present decisions, and so that a better understanding can be gained of the risks to which these decisions are subject. Most companies now use a system of 'rolling' plans, with annual revisions which update and extend the plan.

Figure 5.1 summarises one approach to corporate planning, and is meant to represent a simple one-division company organised on traditional lines under marketing production, etc. The principle applies to the largest multinational, which could be illustrated by inserting boxes representing subsidiaries as well as the departments mentioned. It does not change in concept, regardless of its size, although the operational complexities and the practical problems of strategic choice will increase with the size and diversity of the company. It is obviously simpler and quicker to introduce corporate planning into a one-country, one-market company than into a multinational conglomerate.

Figure 5.1 shows three key elements of strategic planning: the strategies for products and markets (including the opportunities to be exploited and how this will be done), finance, and manpower. These three areas are interrelated, since the available resources of money and people may modify what the company wishes to do, and in some cases stimulate it to do more. Thus a strategy may be devised initially because an opportunity can be clearly seen, or because a surplus of liquid funds dictates a need to find a way of using the money effectively. Strategy will be analysed in more depth later, but for the present it may be stated that strategic planning seeks the answers to questions about how fast the company should grow, what it should do, where, how and when it should do it, and how its present resources should be used and its required resources obtained.

It has already been stated that plans should not be produced in a vacuum. This is emphasised by the three boxes at the top of the diagram, one suggesting pressure from shareholders, and the others the impact of the environment and the company's own analysis of its strengths and weaknesses. Shareholders influence the performance of a

Fig. 5.1 Generalised planning system

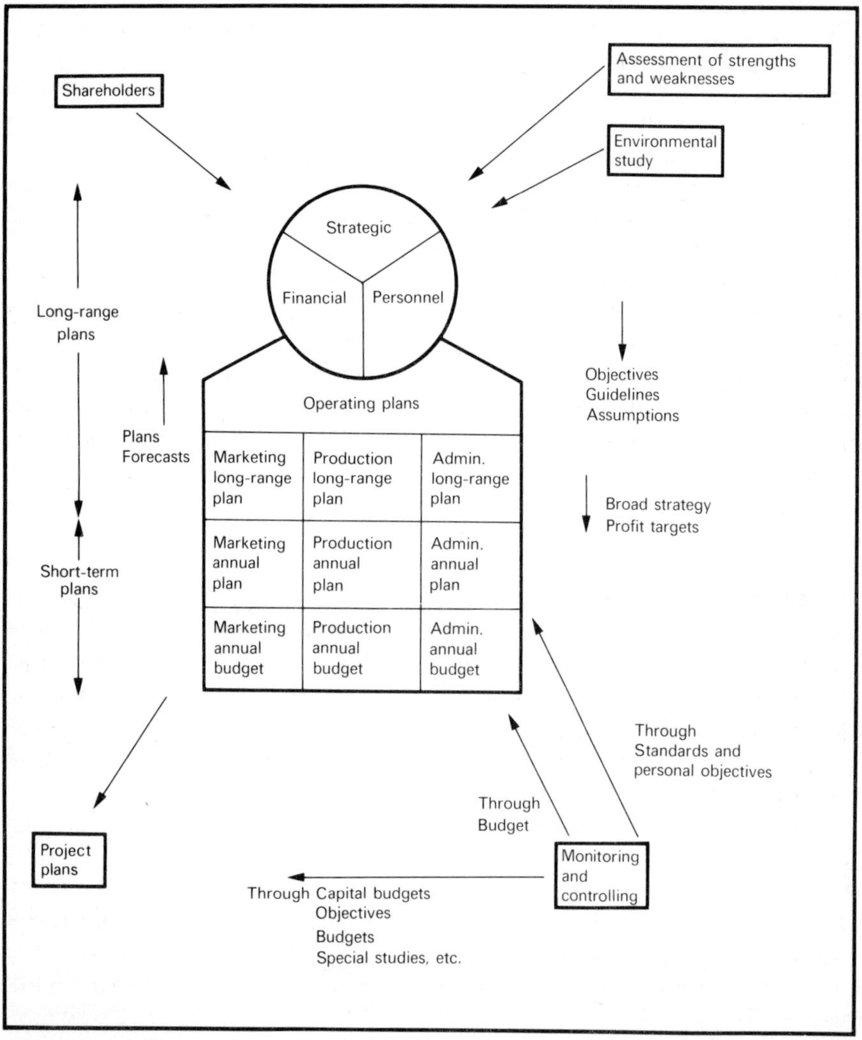

company and through this its objectives. This means that the minimum profit each chief executive tries to achieve is his perception of what the shareholders will find acceptable. With the exception of the family business, where management and owners are either one and the same or likely to be in close contact, it is rarely possible to ask shareholders what they want. Some companies have made the attempt — for example the Fisons Shareholder Survey (Redwood 1971) — and many companies have been made aware by their shareholders that they have failed. Generally it seems reasonable to assume that shareholders require some increase in their returns and a convenient way of measuring this is growth in earnings per share. Although no absolute measure will usually exist of what is an acceptable figure, it is possible to calculate long-term profit objectives for growth in earnings per share, taking into account past trends, results in similar companies and industries, the ambitions of the chief executive, and the expected rate of inflation. Results which lag behind the rate of inflation are hardly likely to prove as exciting to investors, as those which keep ahead of it.

When inflation rates were running at under 8 per cent per year it may not have been too difficult to increase earnings at a higher figure. Inflation at 15 to 20 per cent per year presents a much greater challenge, and it is probable that those companies which practise corporate planning will be setting themselves much tougher targets than those which manage by other means. Unfortunately these targets have to be considered against another environmental factor, price and dividend control, which makes the task of designing strategies to achieve the objectives that much harder.

Modern business can no longer act as if its obligations to shareholders were the only duties it had to accept. There is a growing pressure on business to see itself as a social activity with responsibilities to employees and the community at large. This means that objectives become complicated by constraints and statements of responsibility, which in many ways makes the job of earning profits considerably more difficult. Objectives set in the strategic plan must therefore be modified by the sociopolitical environment, just as the strategies to reach those objectives have to consider these and other factors. This is the reason for the second box in Fig. 5.1 and the pressure which this is shown to be exerting on the company's corporate plans.

The third box demonstrates the pressure on strategy brought about by the company's own limitations and strengths. One of the strong points of corporate planning is that it tries to focus management attention on these issues through a regular process of corporate appraisal. Part of the company strategy might be devoted to correcting some of these weaknesses, and the typical appraisal will also identify opportunities which should be carefully considered. Many companies have found that this process generates sufficient improvement in profits to enable them to embark on their first plan without the need to seek additional strategies. The corporate appraisal should be comprehensive, covering markets, products, facilities, organisation, people and finance, and analysing the risks to which the business is subject.

The planning process considers all these factors at the strategic level, and assesses their impact on the company, its long-term objectives, and the role of each of its activities in the long-term strategy. (More will be said about strategy later.) At this point the company is able to begin to invite the managers of subsidiaries, divisions or departments to contribute their thinking to the long range plan. This may be done in a number of ways, one practicable approach being to issue planning assumptions (as, for example, the rate of inflation to be used in the plan), objectives for each area of the company, and clear policy guide lines. Each activity can analyse its own opportunities and problems within this framework and produce its own long-term plans and forecasts, which are forwarded to corporate headquarters for study, discussion and — once agreement has been reached — incorporation into the total plan of the company.

In preparing these operational plans managers are likely to be faced with the need to coordinate and discuss their plans with the managers of activities which impinge on theirs. Plans should be prepared for a programme which provides for exchange of information and ideas at the right time, so that any problems are either solved or identified for strategic action by the time the plans are complete.

The process of preparing the plans should involve a wide spectrum of people in the company. In a marketing division it would be sensible to have the various product managers prepare the first draft of the plan for their products, rather than this being done by the marketing manager without consultation. Wide involvement increases commitment to the plan, ensures that those closely concerned with specific aspects of the business have a chance to input their knowledge, and provides an opportunity for the cross-fertilisation of ideas.

Eventually a total long-range plan is hammered out for the company. This provides profit targets and standards for the preparation of the annual budget, and ensures that the actions behind the budget figures are compatible with the company's strategies and objectives. The budget thus becomes more meaningful, and it becomes possible to evaluate it against long term intentions, instead of treating it as an isolated event as still happens in many companies. By itself the budget is, of course, a time-proved management tool. It is improved by being linked in this formal way with the long range plans of the company. It is further improved if it is placed in tandem with some form of short-term action plan. The budget and action plan are shown towards the bottom of Fig. 5.1.

The reason for the action plan is simple. Every long-range plan contains a miscellany of things which have to be done if the plan is to succeed. A new product planned for launch two years ahead will only materialise if someone today carries out basic marketing research, if somebody else fulfils a programme of research and development work, and eventually the final product is test marketed before launch. From these three actions spring many more, and failure to implement one of them at the correct time will probably mean that the plan will be found to fail at some future date.

Additionally, things have to be done by people, and one apparently simple strategy in the long-range plan may really be the combined efforts of numerous people from all levels of the organisation. The action plan should define the standards of performance that are required from these various people so that results can be measured. If required this part of the action plan can be developed into a comprehensive system of management by objectives. Either approach will provide a control mechanism which enables a company to monitor activities to be certain that it is implementing its plan, and to see whether the results of these are in any way different from forecast. Where differences appear, management action can be taken, including changing the plan, if necessary.

Budgetary processes will provide part of the necessary monitoring and control. The presence of an action plan should prevent short-term targets from being met only by neglecting necessary development expenditure for the future. Results also have a habit of coming right for the wrong reason and a good action plan will help the budgetary control process to identify when this happens.

The importance of monitoring and control is stressed in Fig. 5.1 by the box in the bottom righthand corner. On the bottom lefthand side is a box showing yet another part of a comprehensive planning process: project analysis and the appraisal of capital expenditure. This represents the detailed evaluation which should take place whenever a major project is identified and before a final commitment is made to that project. Such a need may arise from any of the planning levels shown in the diagram. Projects come in all shapes and sizes, and may cover many different types of decision, such as the acquisition of another company, the launch of a new product, the building of an additional factory, or the installation of replacement plant. Most major strategies planned by the company will give rise to one or more projects. The evaluation of these projects gives the company a chance to confirm that they are still 'right' for the company, to re-examine the financial aspects of a given project, and to produce an action plan for its implementation. Most companies use a fairly careful approach to the appraisal of capital expenditure and discounted cash flow analysis is now commonplace. Projects can be evaluated even if this is the only type of planning the company indulges in but, like budgeting, better results will occur if the projects under appraisal are related to a long-term plan. Besides setting standards, this ensures that resources are committed only when a project is compatible with the company's strategies.

The danger of a formalised approach to planning is that if care is not taken it can become mechanistic. Management involvement in planning can slip into an annual form-filling exercise, about which nobody cares and which makes no real impact on any decisions being taken within the company. This danger becomes particularly prevalent when planning forms are used which call for a mass of detailed accounting information and which resemble the annual budget with a few years tacked on. In this sort of approach it is easy for the company to develop a 'little boxes' mentality where it becomes more important to put a number into each box on the form than to study the causal factors which lie behind the figures.

What corporate planning should do, and what it is capable of doing when wisely and carefully applied, is to stimulate thought and channel personal creativity to the achievement of company objectives. An approach to planning which does not bring about a more creative approach to management is not worth having. Creativity can be encouraged by the way in which people are involved in planning, the type of thought they are asked to put into planning, the sort of information they are expected to produce, the extent to which top management displays an interest in the plans, and the deliberate use of techniques (such as brain-storming) which stimulate creativity, blended with an analytical approach which helps produce the right facts and clearly identifies the issues with which the company is involved.

The practical use of analytical and creative techniques in helping a company to consider inflation and other environmental factors will be demonstrated later. First it is useful to give a few thoughts to the strategic planning process to show some of the aspects which should be considered in the development of a strategic plan.

Fig. 5.2 Gap analysis

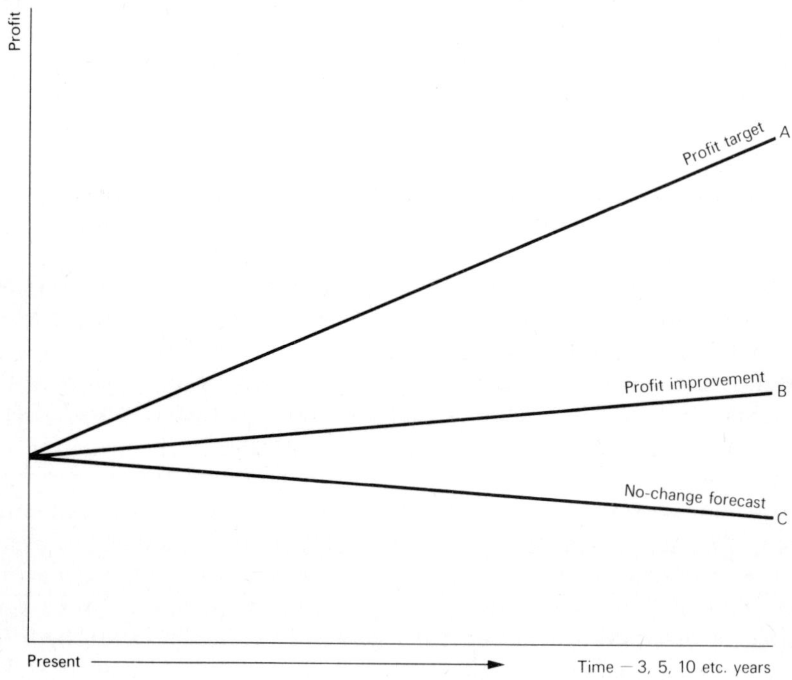

Profit objectives were mentioned in the general description of the corporate planning process. The use of objectives for motivating an organisation is well-known. Figure 5.2 shows, in a simplified form, how profit objectives may be used in the development of strategy. This diagram plots the course to the profit objectives from now to some predetermined date in the future (line A). On the same basis a forecast is made of the future profits to be expected from current activities, assuming the company does nothing to change or add to, those activities. This is represented by line C, suggesting a gradual decline in profits if nothing is done. In fact line C could move in any direction although the chances are that a company adopting a 'do nothing' strategy would steadily worsen its position.

The first line of thought might be how the company might improve the profitability of its present operations. An organisation which has been following a process of corporate planning will find that many of the answers to this question arise from the corporate appraisal. Line B represents the improvement which can be gained in this way, again this line can move in any upward direction and could enable the company to attain the desired level of performance without having to consider other strategies. In most companies an improvement strategy is possible, but requires careful thought, and may require strengthening with continuous effort towards profit improvement (see Chapter 10).

In many companies there will still remain a gap between results forecast after improvement strategies and the profit objective. This gives an indication of the size of the strategic task, and the challenge to management is to find ways of closing that gap. Various courses of action need to be identified which together will bring the company on to its desired course.

Two oversimplifications can be removed. One is that the company is thinking only of the objectives applicable to some future date. Every company also has to think of its short-term position, and part of the skill in planning is to balance short- and long-term requirements. A second simplification is that the company thinks only in terms of profits. From a financial point of view cash flow is more important (although computer assistance is normally required for the development of models to conduct 'gap analysis' in cash flow terms). From a non-financial view the company has many other factors to take into account, not least being various objectives of a social nature which it may feel obliged to meet.

There are many ways of analysing strategy, and all are useful as checklists to help identify possible ways of filling the gap. Overlying whatever approach is selected, should be an appreciation of risk and uncertainty. Most experienced managers know that new projects rarely work out exactly as forecast, and an appreciation of risk and the sensitivity of each project to various changes in assumptions can lead to

Fig. 5.3 Analysis of strategic alternatives

Product	Market	
	Current	New
Current	*(a)*	*(c)*
New	*(b)*	*(d)*

safer and better decision-making. In conditions of uncertain economic circumstances attention to these factors is of paramount importance.

Figure 5.3 provides a simple outline, which forms the basis for a more complex analysis of alternative strategies.

(*a*) *Current products/current markets.* This group of strategies involves improving the performance of the company's present products in the markets they currently serve. It is the sort of problem that marketing men are continually wrestling with, and may evolve from the corporate appraisal and become part of the improvement strategy illustrated in Fig. 5.2. It may arise from a detailed study of the market and environmental factors, and a conviction that there is potential in the area which by definition the company should know best. Improved performance is not measured only by turnover and market share, but by profitability and contribution to the company's objectives. The sort of action which may result from this group of strategies is a change in advertising methods, a new approach to distribution or investment in new production facilities.

(*b*) *New products for current markets.* Next to its own products, a company will know its markets better than anything else. It is logical for the company to investigate things it might do in order to enable it to use its existing distribution facilities to a greater extent. An example of this sort of strategy is the supplier of double-glazing conversion, who adds window modernisation and wall insulation to his products. To the purist of course, any new product has a new market, so for these purposes the market should be defined as the consumers who can be served by existing marketing methods, and these are likely to include many of his present customers.

(*c*) *Current products for new markets.* The strategies of this type sometimes may be self-evident, such as expansion into a new export territory, but more frequently will represent a major challenge to creative thought. Any additional use to which a product can be put can extend its life cycle and add to company profits, with possibilities of gaining worthwhile economies of scale. Simple examples of this type of strategy are the move of an ethical pharmaceutical into the 'over-the-counter' business, or the sale of paints, previously offered only to contractors, to the home decorating market. Crude oil is a product which has been developed into many different markets.

(*d*) *New products for new markets*. Any move into the unknown, however carefully handled, is potentially more dangerous than staying with the known. Diversification is always risky, yet may be essential for the long-term survival of the company.

Fig. 5.4 Strategic choice

Strategy / Method	Existing products for existing markets	New products for existing markets	Existing products for new markets	New products for new markets
Divestment				
Acquisition/Merger				
Research and Development				
Granting licences				
Obtaining licences				
Partnership/Joint venture				
Contract production				
Distribution for others				
Distribution through others				
Selling own essential services				
Hiring staff and starting				
Expansion of existing facilities				

Figure 5.4 takes the analysis a stage further by relating the four types of strategy to the method which might be used to implement the chosen strategies (although not every method is appropriate for every strategy). Every company is faced by a number of options, the choice of which will be influenced by financial and manpower considerations.

The simplest and oldest method is to employ men with necessary skills, purchase or lease the appropriate facilities, and just start. This method is still valid in many circumstances, although it becomes very risky in high capital/high technology industries.

A company may find that the best way to expand is to use somebody else's resources and, possibly, their technological knowledge. Various ways in which this might be done include contract manufacture, the use of another company's distribution facilities, or seeking licences for another firm's products or manufacturing processes. All these courses of action have disadvantages, such as lower potential for long-term profit, less control over one's own future, restrictions in the way opportunities can be exploited, and the problem of matching a current need with available services. Despite this, there are certain major advantages, not least being the reduction of risk of failure, a lessening of the cost penalty for failure, and a saving in capital requirements. From a national point of view such arrangements, although causing some lessening of competition, can bring about a more effective utilisation of resources.

Companies may be seekers of these services. Alternatively they may seek their road to improved profits by actively trying to sell similar arrangements to other companies. The issuing of licences can ensure a greater return from the company's research activity than it could obtain itself, while making its facilities available to perform services for others can be one way of ensuring fuller utilisation of assets

For many years, one of the most popular routes to expansion has been acquisition or merger. This has many obvious advantages, which include the ability to obtain a going concern with an established management, products, manufacturing and distribution facilities thus reducing the lead time of entry into a new area, the avoidance of a profit slump because of the losses which might be made by any other approach, and the financial benefits of mergers which may be attained by an exchange of shares thus avoiding a major requirement for liquid funds. In some cases, such as expansion within present markets, or where heavy capital investment with high risks would be involved, acquisition or merger might be the only realistic way in which a particular strategy could be approached. The drawbacks to acquisition are also very great, and the risks of failure higher than was once commonly realised. In many companies growth by acquisition has been haphazard and unplanned, and the practical problems of the post-acquisition integration of the companies almost completely overlooked.

Partnerships and joint ventures of various kinds reduce the potential rewards, but may also cut down the resource needs, and the risks, provided of course that the partner is chosen wisely. In some countries some form of local equity participation may represent the only way in which a foreign company can establish itself at all.

Research and development may be chosen as the means by which the company expands. This will almost certainly be one of the routes followed by any company of size, particularly if it is involved with high technology or science-based products. No major pharmaceutical company could survive without a substantial investment in research. In some industries, such as aerospace, the costs of necessary research have moved beyond the resources of the individual company and require either Government assistance, or cooperation between companies. Research and development is always difficult to control, and results are hard to predict.

Companies should also consider divestment as a means to growth – although this appears a somewhat paradoxical statement. Although divestment decisions are difficult to make, not least because of the human problem involved, it is essential that companies at least consider getting rid of activities which do not offer long-term profit potential. This may be as simple as dropping a product, or as complex as selling off a subsidiary. Under conditions of severe inflation poor contributing products should be carefully scrutinised and ruthlessly discarded.

None of the items listed will come as a surprise to any manager, and will sound like a catalogue of decisions of which he is fully aware. What is different under a planned approach to management is the attempt to see decisions like these as alternatives, to study them in the light of the environmental situation, and to try to assess not only the full implications of each course of action and probable results, but also the risks to which the decision is exposed. On top of this, the corporate planning approach leads to the creation of many more project ideas, and through their participation in the process, ensures that managers at many levels take account of the issues which surround each decision.

It is absolutely certain that a company which studies its own vulnerability to inflation and assesses future inflationary trends with any degree of realism will make completely different strategies from one which does everything on an unplanned and uncoordinated basis. Examples of the way in which expected future prices of raw materials could change strategic thinking were given in Chapter 1, and are as valid here. In addition the company which considers inflation (and this is taken as only one example of a number of other environmental issues) may find that it seriously changes its expectation of its future sources of funds, deliberately changes to products and markets which appear better opportunities under conditions of severe inflation, avoids investment in the most vulnerable areas and on 'non-essentials' (such as new office furniture), seeks investments that bring cost savings and tries alternatives which take it into new business areas with a low investment (such as licensing).

The gap between objectives and expectations will still be there under inflationary conditions, and in some companies may widen as the costs of high inflation eat into present profits. The challenge to top management to devise appropriate strategies is all the more pressing because the need is greater and the practicable range of choice reduced. This is a reason why the creative and participative aspects of corporate planning are needed even more when conditions are difficult than they are in more normal times.

Identification of the appropriate strategies is only one step in corporate planning. Just as important is the analysis of the changes to which the strategy is sensitive as one method of assessing the vulnerability of the project and the possible alternative approaches to it. All decisions are subject to risk, and no amount of clever analysis can remove all risks. What corporate planning may do is to help identify the extent of most of the risks, so that judgements may be made with greater confidence, and unsafe projects eliminated at an early stage.

There are two main types of risks to which the company may be subject. The first is the risk that every new project has, the chance of partial or complete failure. Assessments of the project may prove to be erroneous, competitive actions may be stronger than expected, forecasts may simply be wrong, or any number of other things may happen. The closer a new strategy is to an existing one, the more chance there is that the company's knowledge and capability will mean that the project is successful. A project which has no relationship to any current activity carries a far greater risk of failure. At the same time the second type of risk may move in an opposite direction. This is the risk to which the business is currently exposed and from which to protect itself the company needs to move into something new. It is the old question of how many eggs to be kept in how many baskets. Often the most pressing strategic need a company can have is to spread its risks in order to secure its long-term future, which may mean the seeking of projects quite different from those it is currently engaged in. When looking at risk from this view the company needs to consider the project very carefully. A diversification into the manufacture of one of its own major raw materials might, for example, involve it in more of the same risks rather than in any way reducing them.

Analysis of risk and sensitivity to adverse factors can be facilitated if a computerised corporate model is used (there are a number of standard packages on the market). Computer assistance is not essential, although it can greatly reduce the labour of analysis and speed up the calculation time. A good model will also allow the feeding in of data once the project is under way, and the analysis of alternatives devised to meet changing conditions.

When conditions are uncertain the need for this sort of analysis becomes much greater, since the risks attached to the project may have increased. Completely flexible plans are an impossibility — it is rarely practicable to halt construction on a half-built factory when all the plant has already been ordered — but nevertheless should be sought.

Contingency plans provide one way of bringing a little more security to an uncertain situation, and can be a logical development to the sensitivity analysis already recommended. The simplest type of contingency plan is the blue-print for an emergency, such as how to maintain communications in the event of a Post Office strike. This type of plan can frequently be completed to a high level of detail, but despite its self-evident significance it will seldom help a company to cope with the sort of problem brought about by a violent change in economic circumstances. What can be of value is a series of less detailed plans, covering significant segments of the corporate plan. In some cases prudence may dictate the need to take hedging actions, or suggest that certain steps might be taken in parallel with the main strategies in order to provide the company with a more secure fall-back position. Thus a British property company, with an adequate portfolio of domestic projects might deliberately substitute, for a few of these, some less profitable projects in another country so that in the event of domestic, political and economic pressure it can more easily direct a greater proportion of its effort into that country. A manufacturer might have embryo plans for marketing a number of substitute products, with a different inflation impact profile, so that if results prove adverse it can speedily redirect its efforts. A cost-reduction strategy might be developed but kept in moth balls so that activities associated with a product which unexpectedly fails can be rapidly cut down to avoid losses. Plans of a similar nature can be prepared for finance, purchasing or virtually any other segment of the total policy.

This investment of time can lead to speedier and more effective decisions at a later date. It is part of the process of preparing the company for the future. Contingency planning, like any other management activity, must be undertaken with judgement. It is patently impossible for any organisation to plan in advance for every possible variation in circumstances: the contingency plans which are made must be chosen with care and cover factors and strategies which are critical to corporate success. No company can expect to have a grand strategy in reserve which can be swung into action the minute its chosen strategy hits problems. Fundamental changes of course are always difficult, and in any case no one is clever enough. Line managers must be encouraged to implement the plans laid and not to think of them as something to be changed at the drop of a hat. Selective contingency planning should, however, be a critical task in strategic management and properly applied may be a powerful tool in the company's struggle to cope with an uncertain future.

Mention has been made of the need for the company to consider the environment as an integral part of the strategic planning process. Chapter 2 touched on the problem of forecasting inflation, and this chapter has already suggested that such forecasts of environmental factors should form a key part of a corporate planning process. The problem is not only the difficulty of making valid forecasts in an uncertain situation, but how to ensure that they really are considered in the planning process. It is all too common for plans to be made regardless of any assessments of the environment, and the same plan would therefore have been made under completely different assessments.

The first step in the process is to study the situation make the forecasts and for working assumptions to be derived from these and agreed by top management. Although it may be difficult to forecast an environmental factor, it is always possible to prepare a logical plan on the basis of any forecast. One can evaluate what to do in a defined set of circumstances, treating as a separate issue what to do if the forecast is wrong. A defined assumption thus enables the company to make plans.

Assumptions also ensure that plans throughout the company are made on a common basis. Any planning assumption is debatable, for however much skill and science is brought to bear on making it, the final answer must be a value judgement. Individual managers will inevitably quarrel with the assumption selected. They must, however, be restrained from following their own inclinations (except in sensitivity analysis and contingency planning) and make all their plans on a common basis. The reasons for this are that the company can quickly see if its assumptions turn out to be incorrect and be aware that changes to plan may be needed — which it could not do if each manager had a different set of assumptions — and can assess centrally the impact of any changes on the main areas of the plan. Although no assumption can be guaranteed to be correct, the one that has been seriously worked on has a greater probability of accuracy, and, as has already been stated, at least the company will know what it is.

There are three major ways of ensuring that the assumption is taken into consideration in the planning stages. Direction, leadership and inspiration from the top will play an important part, and can be demonstrated through planning meetings right through the process, from the setting of the assumption through to the review of the plans by the chief executive. Assumptions that are fully discussed, and their implications aired, will stand more chance of being taken seriously than those which are communicated to managers through a cold and clinical instruction. Similarly, when reviewing their plans, the chief executive will increase his managers' awareness of the problem area if he questions them on the impact of the assumption on their business areas. What have they planned to do about raw material costs? What impact do they consider the expected inflation rate will have on the market and their performance in it? What ways have they come up with to prevent inflation from eating into profits or drying up cash flow?

The second method is analytical, and may be undertaken at various levels in the organisation. Here the analyst tries to understand the impact of the assumption, attempts to answer the sort of question the chief executive should be asking, and gets to grips with the various possible strategies by which the problem can be overcome. Often this sort of examination will reveal areas of ignorance, and may require a positive approach to remove these. Questions about the market impact might lead to marketing research or a comparative study with a similar situation which occurred in another market or in another country. This is perhaps an obvious example from a wide range of possibilities.

In many ways it is the third method which may be the most exciting, as this uses the assumption as a basis from which to develop creative thought. This is by using the planning assumptions as the agenda for a series of company 'brainstorming' meetings, where the participants are required to think positively about the assumptions. If a particular assumption happens, what should the company do? When meetings are set up carefully, with between five to ten participants, made up of people from various functions and varying levels of seniority, this approach can make a significant contribution to the fund of ideas which eventually find their way into the plans. The teams should include people responsible for contributing to the plans, as in this way assumptions are likely to be taken seriously, and the best ideas adopted. Often the approach will help the company to see the opportunities which come with a changing situation, rather than concentrating attention only on the problems.

I hope that this brief description of corporate planning has not suggested that it can be approached in anything but a serious and careful manner. Corporate planning has not been a success for every company which has tried it, and studies of planning successes and failures suggest that this is frequently because of the way in which the company approaches it. Corporate planning is frequently given superficial attention by those who should be most concerned with it, top management, and expected to flourish like a technique which can be called upon at will, and which is not integrated with any aspect of day to day management. Where this is accompanied by an indifference to any possibilities that change the *status quo*, and a confusion of planning with forecasting, budgeting, computer models or some other technique, any attempt to plan is predestined to fail. Many companies with so-called 'planning departments' do not plan. If any general criticism can be levelled at British industry it is that 'planning' has too often been concerned with internally generated accounting data, and too seldom takes note of any possible changes generated by forces outside the company. No general criticism is ever really fair, and there are exceptions, but the fact remains that corporate planning requires a particular attitude of mind by the chief executive and his board to create a climate in which it can develop. A willingness to consider and confront change, and a reasonable investment of the time of managers at all levels. On top of this the company must possess or obtain the basic skill and knowledge to make planning work.

If these factors are present, corporate planning can become a most effective weapon with which to face an increasingly difficult and uncertain world. Most weapons are only useful when in skilled hands; for those who only play with them they may be a source of danger. The conclusion is self-evident: those who are willing to approach it properly should seriously consider corporate planning: those who already use it should overhaul their approach to reassure themselves that they belong to that minority of companies which is planning sensibly and effectively.

The weapon is available, its methods are well documented and its ability to succeed well proven. But no one can help the company which deliberately refuses to open its eyes.

References and further reading

ACKOFF, R. C. (1970) *A concept of Corporate Planning*, Wiley Interscience.

ANSOFF, H. I. (1965) *Corporate Strategy*, McGraw-Hill.

BAYNES, P. (ed.) (1973) *Case Studies in Corporate Planning*, Pitman.

HUSSEY, D. E. (1971) *Introducing Corporate Planning*, Pergamon.

HUSSEY, D. E. (1974) *Corporate Planning: theory and practice*, Pergamon.

HUSSEY, D. E. (ed.) (1974) *Corporate Planners Yearbook 1974/5*, Pergamon.

REDWOOD, H. (1971) The Fisons Shareholder Survey, *Long Range Planning*, April.

STEINER, G. A. (1969) *Top Management Planning*, Macmillan.

WARREN, E. K. (1966) *Long-Range Planning: the executive viewpoint*, Prentice Hall.

6

Further implications for planning and accounting

One issue that has long engaged the attention of planners, economists and accountants is whether to plan in current or constant prices. Many corporate plans are prepared on the basis of today's prices. The preceding chapters have made my views clear. I can see no merit in pretending that inflation does not exist, for to ignore an essential element of modern business is hardly a recipe for successful planning. On the other hand a planning formula which merely consists of grossing up all figures by the same inflation index is hardly any better. In many company plans the only mention of inflation is one line which states which rate has been used for each year of the plan. Anyone who poses this question about plans is asking the unanswerable, since it is nonsense to assume that the same rate applies to all costs, all selling prices and all products.

Giving consideration to inflation means doing what has been argued in previous chapters: analysing the effect on costs, prices, products and markets, and on financial and human resources. Thus the amount by which figures may change because of inflation is rarely a constant right across the board, and the fact of inflation will usually lead to different strategies which would simply not appear in any form of constant price planning.

The essence of good planning is to take account of changing circumstances. It is not just an exercise in extrapolating the present into the future. Companies which ignore inflation cannot be planning efficiently: the higher the rate of inflation the less effective will their plans be.

Apart from the fact that to ignore inflation is to fail in planning, constant prices plans suffer from another problem: they become next to impossible to monitor. Post-auditing of results against plans becomes so difficult that, even with annual revision, it is hard to be sure that the original intentions are being carried out.

A similar controversy has found its way into capital expenditure appraisal, particularly when the d.c.f. (discounted cash flow) method is used. Although many of the writings on d.c.f. ignore the whole question of inflation, others specifically suggest that it be ignored. For example, the National Economic Development Council (1971, p. 11) states:

> It is sometimes argued that in estimating the expected costs and revenues for a project allowance should be made for the effects of any general inflation of the price level anticipated during the life of the project. This is a complex problem but since general inflation can be expected to have a similar effect on both costs and revenues there is no need to build its impact into the calculation of the cash flow, so long as the cash flow is discounted by the real cost of finance. It is necessary however to take account of changes in relative prices and costs where it is expected that the movements of prices and costs of relevance to the particular investment decision are likely to differ from the inflation of prices and costs in general.

My view is that the exception in the above quotation is always the rule, and inflation should never be ignored.

In the evaluation of capital expenditure projects there are three groups of factors to be considered: monitoring (or auditing), the assessment of the expected results, and the rate of discount to be used. The first two have many similarities with the points already made about inflation in corporate plans, the last is unique to d.c.f. analysis.

The monitoring problem becomes particularly apparent in capital expenditure appraisal because the lag in many projects between cash outflows and inflows gives an opportunity for inflation to bite. For example, a new factory may take two to three years to build and bring into production, and revenue may not flow back to the project from sales until well into the third year, at which time both costs and prices will be very different from any assumed in a constant price calculation. This difficulty can be partly alleviated by expressing as much of the project as possible in physical output units (weight of product, hours of production, number of employees) and this should be done. But in the final event the purpose of monitoring is to ascertain whether a project has contributed to profits and cash flow in the way originally intended. The need for this is neither for criticism nor self-congratulation; it is to provide early warning so that projects can be modified and errors corrected, and to enable the company to learn from its experiences.

Life would be very much simpler if the common assumption about inflation, which is repeated in the NEDC quotation above, were correct. In fact inflation is likely to change any or all of the inputs into the d.c.f. analysis: fixed capital, working capital, all elements of unit costs, selling price, taxation, and the volume of sales and therefore production.

Like corporate plans, project appraisals should study the impact of inflation in detail, seeking both to quantify its effects, and to understand how it might cause changes in the way a project is planned. This will involve a deep knowledge of the market, particularly the likely demand curve, and competitive or Government reactions to various price structures. In other words, the average project will need adequate market research and careful forecasting, probably to a higher standard than most companies usually allow. With the alternative price/volume forecasts should be considered the different marketing strategies (and their costs) which may be applied. If, for market or legal reasons, price rises lag behind cost rises this must also be considered. On the cost side a forecast should be developed of price trends of labour and major raw materials for each of the main products in the project, as well as price trends for those overheads incurred by the project.

It is also important that assumptions used throughout the company are on a common basis, preferably tied to the corporate planning activity. The impact of the assumptions will vary from project to project. One of the main values of the d.c.f. method is that it allows a standard quantitative comparison of alternatives within a project, and of one project with another. Thus it is a particularly useful tool in a capital rationing situation. If assumptions differ between alternatives or projects this common basis of comparison will be lost, and decisions based on the net present values (n.p.v.) and d.c.f. rates may be invalid.

This presents analysts, particularly in a large company, with an additional problem, and partly explains why the 'inflation may be ignored' policy is so popular. Here at least all projects are known to be on a common basis, the only problem is that the data inputs to the project are very likely to be wrong. Because all projects are uncertain, sensitivity analysis should be carried out, and 'what if' questions raised. As with the corporate plan, this sort of analysis can be made easier if some form of computer assistance is used. Many bureaux now offer suitable packages so that this sort of analysis is within the reach of even the smallest company.

Inevitably, much of what has been written about d.c.f. has concentrated on the mathematics of the method. It has always been true that no analysis, however complex, can be meaningful unless the basic data of the project has validity. An inflationary situation calls for even more care in establishing the basic facts and forecasts on which the analysis is based. Inflation makes it harder, which means that more care and more effort should be given to the basic studies. And this need is present whether the company uses the most sophisticated methods of d.c.f. or relies on the traditional and less effective methods such as return on investment and payback.

The third issue which arises in d.c.f. under inflationary conditions is the required rate of return at which the project should be discounted. The rate is used in two possible ways: as the basis on which to calculate the net present value (n.p.v.), or to indicate the minimum rate which is acceptable, any projects failing to achieve this being automatically rejected.

Much has been written about the selection of the required rate of return, but the essence of the basic principle has been concisely stated by NEDC (1971, pp. 17–18):

> In the first place it is clearly important that companies should not invest in projects which are expected to give a return less than the return which it thought can be achieved from other forms of investment. For example, if it is expected that a return of 8 per cent in real terms (i.e. after allowing for inflation) after corporation tax (but gross of income tax) can be earned by investing in equities, a company will fail to maximise its projects if it chooses instead to invest in a project of its own which has a real return of less than 8 per cent after corporation tax. Therefore to act in the best interests of shareholders, a company should require a return at least as great as the highest return, after taking into account differences in risk which can be obtained from alternative forms of investment.
>
> Secondly, a company should also require a return from a new investment at least as great as its marginal cost of finance, otherwise it is not only unlikely that maximum profits will be earned for shareholders, but also losses may be incurred.

One school of thought argues that general rates of returns are in fact adjusted for inflation by the forces of the market, and that the marginal cost of finance will therefore reflect the correct amount of inflation. This is only true in so far as Government policy allows it to be. Another view is that the required rate of return should be specifically adjusted by the rate of inflation used in the project, but this appears to be related to the theory that inflation strikes all parts of the project at the same general rate. I have already shown the faults of this approach.

My view is that the rate of inflation should influence the required rate of return, not through any simple formula, but because it has an effect on the expected future costs of finance. The expected results of any project are the combination of a series of forecasts: the marginal costs of financing those results should also be a forecast. Using today's rates without thought, for a project which has to be financed in the future can be as dangerous as adding an inflation element to today's rate, when the forces which determine financial costs are much more complex than inflation alone. There is no guarantee that any company will forecast its rate correctly, and if conditions are very uncertain a higher rate should be required to compensate for the extra risks involved.

In the final event the best d.c.f. analysis is only a guide for management, and nothing can take away the element of judgement which management has to use in its final decisions.

Capital investment appraisal is not the only area where the approach used by the company may be inadequate for modern conditions. Many costing systems, which have proved their worth in times of relatively low inflation and freedom in pricing decisions, simply do not work effectively when inflation rates are very high or uncertain, or when there are legal restrictions on price increases.

Standard costing is probably the commonest approach, although there are companies which continue to apply various forms of historical costing. Sizer (1969, p. 70) states: 'In a standard costing system *predetermined* costs are carefully computed and later contrasted with actual costs to aid in cost control. The difference between the actual costs and the predetermined standard costs are called variances. The cost accountant analyses these variances by causes and inefficiencies are promptly notified to the persons responsible for them.' This sums up the essence of standard costing.

Companies vary in their approach to costing, and many practise absorption costing, where all costs are allocated in accordance with the 'normal', or planned, volume of output. Others practice marginal costing, and do not allocate overheads. A flexible budgeting approach may be used in conjunction with absorption costing, in order that overheads may be more accurately allocated when volumes are above or below the normal. The objectives of a costing system are defined by Taylor (1974, p. 8) to be:

1 To assist managers in their function of forward planning and controlling the operations for which they are responsible.
2 To assist in the determination of price and pricing policy.
3 To value work in progress and stocks as an essential element in the accounting process of profit ascertainment.

The method of costing chosen will affect the way in which these objectives are achieved, and may have a particular impact on pricing decisions. Prices based on contribution are likely to be quite different from prices based on absorption costs, while even within an absorption system the methods which have to be chosen, quite arbitrarily, for allocating overheads may also result in a different price structure. Costing is not the same as pricing, although there are strong links between the two.

Typically, standard costs are set (usually associated with the annual budget) to cover a twelve-month period. Expected prices for labour and raw materials are built into the costs. If the forecasts are right the

Fig. 6.1 Standard costs and high/low inflation

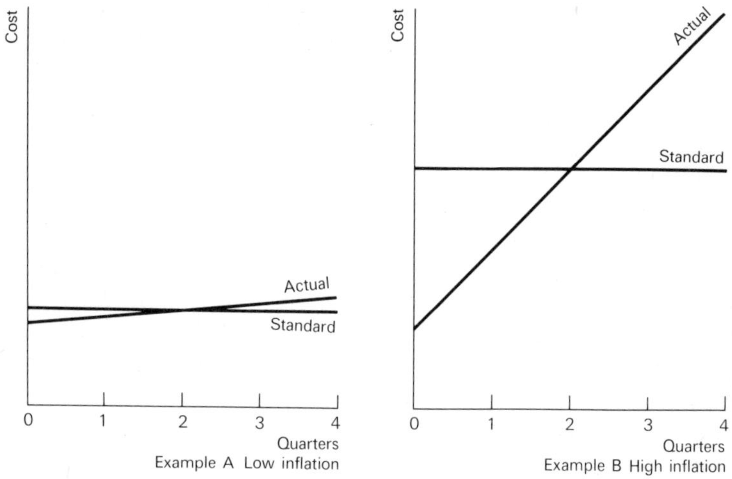

expectation is that the company will over-recover for inflation in the first period of the year, and under-recover for the second, so that on average the company fully recovers its additional costs over the whole period. This is illustrated in Fig. 6.1, which shows two raw material cost lines, one at a low rate and the other at a high rate. To simplify the diagram equal monthly volumes and cost rises have been assumed. These have been compared with a standard cost line which smooths out the increase, the area of surplus at the beginning equalling the area of deficit at the end.

Typically, costs will be revised at the end of the year and the new standards computed will be used as a basis for pricing decisions. Many companies appear to carry out this review in January, and the effect is so marked that it has an impact on national statistics. *Economic Trends* (1974) writing on the 'index of wholesale prices of basic materials and fuels purchased by industry' observes: 'This index normally rises at about twice the average monthly rate in January, reflecting the timing of periodic price reviews by many manufacturers.'

When the rate of inflation is relatively low (example A of Fig. 6.1) the degree of overpricing at the beginning of the period is also low, as is the risk that the estimates are wrong. Under high inflation (example B) product prices can be too high at the beginning of the period, and too low at the end, unless a more flexible pricing policy is adopted. The risks involved are also greater, although in theory the company can always adjust prices upwards if variances indicate the need to do this. The requirements are for speedy and accurate reporting against standards, information about variances and statutory freedom to adjust prices as required.

Fig. 6.2 Principal cost variances

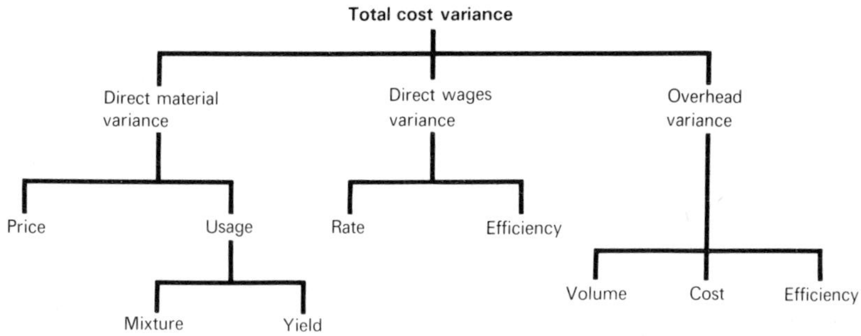

The question of pricing is taken up again in the next chapter, for there is more to be said. What needs to be assessed here is whether the normal costing system can give the speedy response required under conditions of high inflation, particularly in the more usual business situation where inflation does not strike in regular monthly increments, and where volume may not be the same each month.

Sizer (1969, p. 73) provides the statement of principal cost variances reproduced in Fig. 6.2. Of the many variances illustrated three are directly affected by inflation: the price of raw materials, the rate for direct labour, and the cost of overheads. Raw materials may also show a variance because of buying inefficiencies, or unexpected increases in production which necessitate purchasing emergency supplies.

A major task of the cost accountant is to identify and report on the variances and their apparent cause. In a time of high inflation this approach has two major weaknesses: the timeliness of reporting and the fact that price increases may not trigger a variance report early enough for action. By definition a variance report can only be prepared at the end of a period, and after costs have been incurred. The variance report therefore compares a slice of history with the standard. In addition to the fact that it reports on the past, there is a further timelag during which the accountants analyse the data, prepare the report, and subsequently while the appropriate managers study the report and decide what action to take.

Because positive variances are expected during the first part of the year, in theory being eroded to nothing by the year end, a major adverse trend may remain unnoticed for a number of reporting periods. This may mean that at these points the company will be producing within its standard costs, but that by the end of the year these will be exceeded. Such a situation is more likely to arise with raw materials than with the labour rate, since the former is typically the combination of numerous transactions, while changes in labour rates are likely to be the result of a few negotiated and widely known adjustments.

Companies which set a standard price for each raw material and monitor this separately will be more likely to notice adverse changes in prices of individual raw materials, although again a faster-than-expected rate of change may escape unnoticed.

These two factors may mean that alarm bells to suggest that price should be re-examined do not ring until too late, price action is delayed, and total profit contribution reduced. Where legislation requires submission of a price increase to a Government body for approval, additional delays will occur. Early warning might have enabled more speedy action to be taken.

Ways of improving this situation are either to reassess standard costs at more frequent intervals than the normal year, or to devise a monitoring tool which will ring those alarm bells when inflation escapes the variance report. The first solution can easily become administratively unworkable, and in any case would still suffer from the delays in reporting variances. The second offers considerable opportunity, and can be applied through the development of indices to measure inflation. Before examining how such a tool might be developed and used, it is as well to spend a little time considering the various types of inflation and the indices that can be used to measure them.

National inflation has numerous facets, all of which are interrelated, but which do not have a uniform impact on all economic activity. Examples of some of the various indices were given in Chapter 1, and reference is made to these figures where appropriate.

Retail prices. Perhaps the most commonly quoted measure of inflation is the retail price index (see Fig. 1.4) which assesses changes in retail prices as they affect the consumer. It is widely used as a monitor of the general level of inflation, and because it measures consumer prices, is frequently quoted in the press, and used as a basis of wage negotiations. Its main defect is that it measures an average state, and neither the prices observed nor the weightings given to them will fairly represent the situation of every individual consumer. In the UK the details of how the index is constructed are published, as is a breakdown of the index into categories, such as food, alcoholic drink, and housing. It provides an invaluable measure of inflation, and has a most important influence on political and economic policies, and public opinion. In no way should it be used as a general inflation adjustment factor in the forward planning of individual companies, although it is widely misused in this way.

Consumers' expenditure deflator. A second measure of the impact of inflation on all consumers is the implied price index for all consumer's expenditure, which can in the UK be derived from the national income accounts. The attraction of this index is that it measures the total expenditure of all consumers: its weakness is that, unlike the narrower retail prices index which appears monthly, it is only published at yearly intervals and is subject to revision in future years. It thus has certain practical restrictions which stop it from being used as a dynamic measure of inflation.

Wholesale prices. In the UK two other series of indices measure inflation at a different level. One analyses the cost of materials and fuels purchased by broad sectors of industry: food, chemicals, steel, mechanical engineering, electrical engineering, electrical machinery, textiles, clothing, timber, paper, construction and building materials. The other measures the price charged for the output of a basically similar list of broad industry sectors (see Table 1.3).

Within their limitations these two sets of indices provide a much better base from which to study the impact of inflation on individual firms and their competitors. Both are published monthly, although anyone who uses them would be well advised to study how they are compiled, since the usefulness to a particular business must be affected by the definitions of the industry sectors, the prices sampled, the time of the month when they are sampled, and the weightings given to each factor. Few companies will find that their own purchases of fuel and materials are identical by type and proportion with the index.

Commodity prices. From official and private sources trends of prices of individual commodities and products can be calculated. These in no way measure the general level of inflation, although they are of value in certain situations or for specific businesses.

Wages. The other side of the inflation coin is wages, and there are a number of indices which monitor wage inflation on a national and/or industry basis. For example, the UK publishes series which measure the weekly rates of wages for manual workers, average earnings of employees, income per man-hour, and wages and salaries per unit of output. The last series will, of course, offset some of the costs of inflation to gains in productivity. Wage indices are widely publicised and because they are available on a monthly basis, greatly influence economic policy. The more specific indices are of greater value in examining the impact of inflation on individual businesses (although subject to the limitations of each index) than any measure of national inflation.

Internal company inflation. So much for the national statistics which measure inflation. At any one time the total inflation rate of the individual company may differ from the national picture, and is a weighted average of the numerous inflation rates which apply. Traditionally the internal rate of inflation is calculated when the annual budget is put together, and the different factors which make up the total expense are analysed and rates of increase considered.

The fact that none of the national measures of inflation can be guaranteed to give answers which apply to individual firms, leads to the suggestion that companies calculate their own raw material and labour rates indices. These can become a tool which, when used in conjunction with the standard costs, will partly alleviate those disadvantages of costing systems discussed earlier in this chapter.

A raw materials index has particular advantages, as it can be based on commitments. The buyer is normally aware of price increases some weeks before the cost accountant, since he knows when placing the order, whereas the accountant only knows after the goods have been delivered and the paperwork passed through the system. Thus the first advantage an index will have is that it will give speedier information about raw material cost increases.

The second advantage is that a month by month forecast of the raw materials index can be prepared in a way which is compatible with the standard costs. The actual index can be monitored quickly and regularly against this, the 'standard' index for the year entered, and it can easily be seen whether inflation is moving faster than originally expected, thus removing the difficulty of observing inflation trends when the standard cost variance is still positive.

Similar arguments can be presented for a productive labour rate index. It is also possible to combine this with the raw materials index into a 'factors of production' index: again to obtain a clearer and earlier indication of trends. None of these indices will tell the company what its costs are, since they only measure the inflation elements of the numerous variances shown in Fig. 6.2. but they do set the right alarm bells ringing so that action can be taken, where it is needed, much earlier than would have otherwise been possible.

The company's own indices can be as complicated as those used by Government, and can be based on the principles and rules (which are published) used by Government in the calculation of these indices. In most cases simpler and less detailed methods are quite adequate. A simpler method for calculating a raw materials index is:

1 Analyse all raw material purchases into basically similar groups: for example copper, steel, electronic components, or whatever is relevant to the company.
2 Select from each group one or two of the most important items to be used as indicators.
3 Establish a 'standard' price for the year for each of these indicators in conjunction with the standard costing system.
4 On the same day each month record the current commitment price of each of the indicators.
5 An index may then be created for each raw material group, using the

indicator data, and establishing an appropriate base data for the series.

6 Establish weighting factors for each raw material group for (*a*) total raw material usage, and (*b*) each major product for which an index is to be created. (The selection of products should be chosen with care, combined where possible into groups and covering the major products only.)
7 Apply the appropriate weighting factor to the prices obtained for each indicator, and obtain the weighted average raw material costs for (*a*) all raw materials and (*b*) the selected products.
8 Index these costs to the base date.

The index can be compared, possibly graphically, with the forecast index and the point in the forthcoming year when the standard cost of raw materials is reached can also be marked. (Chapter 8 deals in more depth with organising to make better forecasts of raw material prices.)

Labour rates indices can, in their simplest form, be based on changes in rates, either through settlements or threshold payments, and ignore changes in the mix of grades of labour. Forecasts of future indices will show changes caused by expected settlements and the expected threshold triggers. An index compatible with the raw materials index can easily be constructed. Where necessary separate indices may be created for different types of labour, and combined in the correct proportions for either the total company or specific products.

The 'factors of production' index can be made on a total company, or product, basis by calculating the appropriate weighting factors for labour and raw materials and using these to produce the combined index. (It may also be necessary to allow a timelag in the raw materials index.) This tool helps the company to see where it stands in the inflation game, at least as far as costs are concerned. It also helps it to compare what is happening with its budget or plan for what it expected to happen. This enables it to see if additional action is required more clearly and much faster than if it relied only on variance analysis of standard costs. The indices can also be part of a dynamic forecasting system, under which expectations for the future are continually reassessed, and the impact on price strategies properly studied.

The approaches outlined in this chapter will put the company in a better position to make the right decisions in an inflationary situation. They will not, of course, automatically ensure that the company will make correct decisions, and there are many further strategic implications to be considered in later chapters.

References

NATIONAL ECONOMIC DEVELOPMENT COUNCIL (1971) *Investment Appraisal*, HMSO.

SIZER, J. (1969) *An Insight into Management Accounting*, Penguin.
TAYLOR, A. H. (1974) *Costing: A Management Approach*, Pan, p. 8.
CENTRAL STATISTICAL OFFICE (1974) 'The economic situation', *Economic Trends*, HMSO, no. 244, February, p. vi.

7

Further strategic considerations

Chapter 6 dealt at some length with cost, and the vital need for timely indication of inflationary trends. Although costing data may be a key element in pricing decisions, the determination of prices is very much a matter of marketing. The marketing task is to satisfy consumer needs in a way which will yield the company its required level of profits. It is easy to give the consumer what he wants, but difficult even at the best of times to do so in a way which also satisfies the company. Under conditions of high inflation this task may become exceedingly difficult, and worse than difficult when the company's freedom to act is curtailed by some form of anti-inflation legislation.

Inflation makes greater demands on marketing skills. Enough has been said elsewhere to demonstrate my contention that when inflationary increases are high they can rarely be passed on as price increases without there being some effect on the market. Under these conditions marketing management has to face the challenge of either devising a strategy which overcomes the impact on the market of the price change, or to find some other way of meeting the company's profit requirements. The additional demands that violently changing conditions make on market research were mentioned in the discussion on project analysis in Chapter 6.

Even if the assessment of the market suggests that it is capable of absorbing price increases, the strategy under conditions of high inflation requires considerable thought.

Figure 7.1 illustrates a situation where a new standard cost is computed (C2) which shows a considerable increase over the standard for the previous year (C1). It is assumed for these purposes that the standard can be accurately forecast and that the organisation intends to raise prices so that the total year's trading yields the same contribution as in the preceding year. The figure shows four of the many pricing possibilities that the marketing manager might consider.

Fig. 7.1 Alternative price strategies and effect on subsequent year

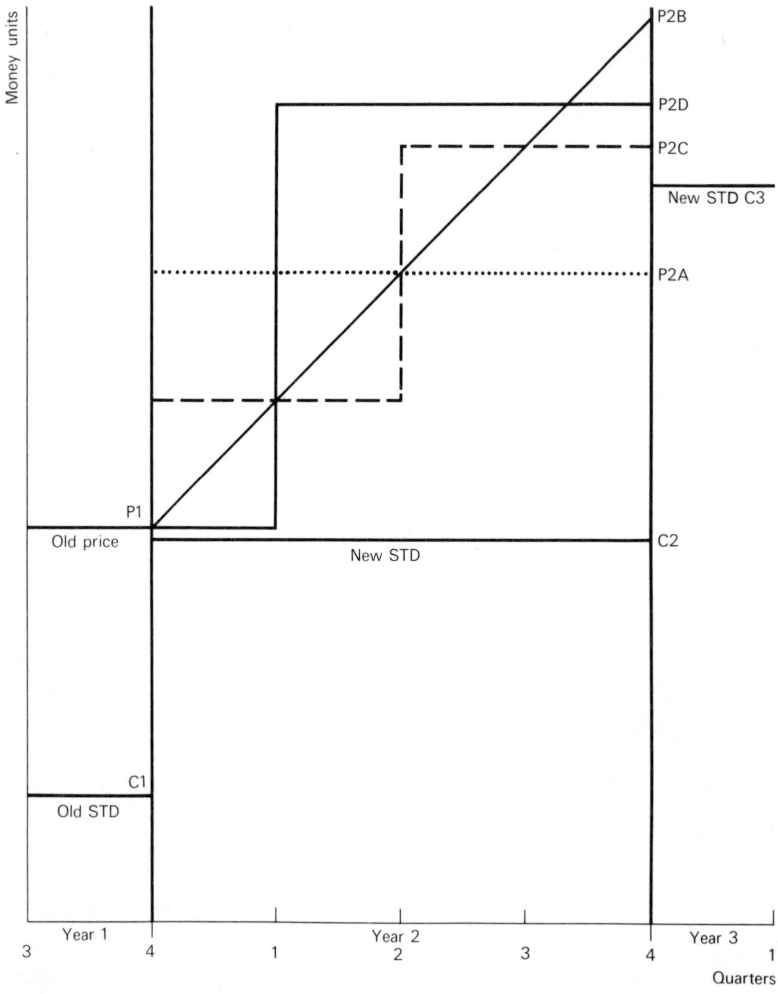

Line A Option 1. Increase price at the same rate as the cost increase and hold for twelve months

The effect of this strategy would be to overprice the product at the beginning of the period and to underprice it at the end.

Line B Option 2. Increase price by an equal amount each month

Assuming real costs more evenly through the year, this will mean that cost and price inflation keep in step.

Line C Option 3. Increase price in two steps

Under this option the initial price increase would not be as high as in Option 1. However the second price would have to be higher if the same average price were to result at the end of the year.

Line D **Option 4. Make no price increase for three months and then make one increase**

Because none of the increase costs have been recovered for the first part of the year, the price increase, when it is made has to recover the lost profits as well as provide the right amount of revenue for the remaining nine months of the year.

The marketing manager in this example has based his calculations on an intention to sell an equal volume of product each month. Even if the market could stand some price increases it is obvious that the chance of this volume assumption being right is different in each of the options. What is more likely to happen is that he will sell too much at the lower prices and too little at the higher, thus affecting his total realisation.

But there is another important implication. Assume that standard costs rise by an equal amount in the following year. Depending on which price strategy has been adopted this year will be the amount of increase needed in prices. The difference between these possible year end prices are significant — and, of course, there are many other possible price strategies which would have given different answers.

There is nothing new about these observations, and the same pattern applies whatever the rate of inflation. When inflation is under 5 per cent per year the money differences in price under the alternative strategies are tolerable, at least between the strategies that the company is most likely to adopt. When costs rise by, for example, 15 to 20 per cent per year the money differences in price may be embarrassingly significant.

The implication of Fig. 7.1 is that in addition to all the problems of assessing his price strategy against the market and profit criteria, heavy inflation causes the marketing manager to have a greater concern with the longer-term implication of his decisions than perhaps he does when inflation rates are low. It also goes without saying that the penalty of wrong decisions can be greater when inflation rates are high. This echoes the message of the last chapter, and the need to be aware when actual costs have changed compared to the standards.

One method of pricing which gives the company some protection against inflation is to build an escalation or price variation clause into the contract. This is particularly important in construction and engineering, where there is a significant length of time between booking an order and fulfilling it. Usually such pricing strategies provide the vendor with a measure of protection against price increases which are difficult to forecast, sometimes through some form of indexation. That there is a need for such protection is demonstrated by the Concorde forecasts in Table 1.1.

The Building Economic Development Council (1974, p. 2) summarises the differences between the two principal methods of adjusting for price variations.

> It is important to appreciate the fundamental difference between calculating the reimbursement of fluctuations (rise or fall) on a limited range of actual costs and the amount assessed under formula methods.
> (*a*) With actual costs, reimbursement is a net amount calculated from wages sheets, invoices and the like in accordance with the appropriate provisions of the contract. Likewise, the general contractor can usually recover the net extra he has paid to his unnominated sub-contractors in respect of price fluctuations. Reimbursement of fluctuations in materials can be restricted to a basic list, and there is no specific reimbursement for overheads and profit, unless otherwise provided for in the contract.
> (*b*) Formula methods involve recovery only against changes in the indices. For items subject to formula recovering, individual costs included in the build up of a tender are not used in the calculation of reimbursements. There is no need, therefore to specify the materials subject to fluctuation provision, no need to submit a list of basic prices and no need to take into account promulgated future changes. Formulae reimbursement results from changes in the indices as from the base index defined in the contract documents, quite irrespective of the actual costs (or savings) incurred by the contractor, or sub-contractor.
> . . . it will be seen that there is a saving in the effort currently devoted by the contractor's staff to submitting detailed evidence of each price change, and that of the surveyor's or client's staff in agreeing these, and of audit staff in checking them. However, more work is involved for quantity surveyors at both the pre-contract and post-contract stages.

The same report provides formulae for thirty-four categories of building work — for example (1) demolition, site preparation, excavation and disposal, (2) hardcore and imported filling, (3) piling — and for certain specialist engineering functions (electrical, heating, ventilating, air conditioning, lift installation and structural steel work).

The appendices to this chapter give examples of each of the price variation methods. Appendix 1 shows the formula method of the National Association of Lift Manufacturers. Appendix 2 gives the appropriate 'fluctuation' clauses of the standard contract of the Joint Contracts Tribunal which is based on the actual variation method.

During 1974 a number of manufacturers attempted to introduce price variation clauses into their contracts: this practice was prevented, except in industries which had traditionally applied escalation clauses, by the anti-inflation legislation. Nevertheless, the possibility may be worth examining in the future by any company that has a significant delay between taking an order and fulfilling it. The ability to introduce such clauses depends, of course, on the relative strengths of vendors and buyers. It seems a fair approach for all parties.

Pricing decisions can be difficult in any conditions, and next to impossible when costs are increasing rapidly and by large amounts. Some of the problems of keeping up to date with costs were discussed in the previous chapter. Pricing decisions depend on more than an up-to-date knowledge of the market and of movements in costs: they require a complete understanding of the basis of the company's costing system. This is not the forum for yet another voice in the ceaseless argument over the merits and demerits of absorption and contribution costing systems. What is important is for those making pricing decisions to appreciate the effect on costs which are brought about by changing demand patterns. An increase in sales volume may lead to lower unit costs. On the other hand, if a price increase leads to lower sales, there may be a rise in unit costs which means that profit margins are eroded further. In addition to the potential impact on demand of price increases, the marketing manager should appraise the effect of inflation on direct competitors and on substitutes. Chapter 1 argued that inflation rarely strikes evenly across different companies and industries. The reaction of the effected organisations to the impact of inflation are also different. Although a competitor's price strategy and cost structure can provide a threat, the bigger enemy may be the substitute. This can work in reverse, too, and may provide an opportunity for the aggressive marketing manager to exploit.

When price structures alter significantly, it is time to review all elements of the marketing strategy, including the most basic question of all. Is this product right for tomorrow's market? 'Right' means not only does the consumer want it, but will he buy it at a price which gives the company its required level of profit? If inflation has made the product 'wrong' the company has three possible solutions:

- to continue selling, despite the fact that either price or volume are too low to give adequate profits;
- to amend the product so that it can meet both consumer and profit requirements (this may be by changes to the physical composition of the product, the raw materials which go into it, the process of manufacture, the packaging, or the invisible part of the product — guarantees, consumer service or credit);
- to change the product mix, either by complete withdrawal of the offending product, or by deliberately reducing the quantity offered for sale (a change in product mix implies the substitution of a more profitable product).

Each of these solutions may imply a reconsideration of promotion and distribution strategies. For example it may be desirable to positively promote a changed product through increased advertising: a reduction in quantity offered for sale might be supported by an increase in price and withdrawal of promotion.

Each solution will also have its own impact on the total strategy of the company, directly because of its effect on production and cash flow, and indirectly because of the way it will alter investment, research and development and the company's whole approach to expansion and growth. An appreciation of the broader effect of each solution can lead the company to change its priorities and future intentions.

In the longer term the first suggested solution is likely to be untenable, since no sensible company will continue to support unprofitable products. As a short-term solution it may be justifiable: if, for example, the assessment is that the market will stand an adequate price increase in the near future, or as a short-term approach while research and development produce a modified product which will enable a switch to be made to the second solutions. Anti-inflation legislation may force a company into the 'no action' solution at least for a short period where, for example, there has to be an interval of three months between applications for price increases.

In many ways the second solution, if it is a possibility for the particular product in question, is the best, and certainly the least inflationary (Chapters 8 and 10 deal more specifically with certain of the areas of cost). However, by their nature, many of these possible solutions may take a long time to develop. This is a strong argument for both planning and control, since in this sort of situation any additional lead time which can be gained may provide the opportunity for work to be carried out and for ideas to be tested.

The third solution is easier to offer than to apply, and in extreme cases may involve the company in disinvestment decisions or in redundancies. Any company can, if it wishes, drop a product from its list (although even this may be difficult in certain situations: the public relations effect on a pharmaceutical company which withdraws a life-saving drug, or on the domestic electrical company where a failure to supply spares for one product could seriously harm its reputation for after-sales service for all other products). Only flexible companies can manipulate the product mix so that products are expanded or declined at will. Lietaer (1970, p. 117) states that:

> Adjusting the product mix has been an escape hatch for many corporations confronted with hyperinflation and drastic price controls. Specifically, it has been a key ingredient of the strategy of Merck, Sharp and Dohme Industria Quimica and Farmaceutica S.A., an affiliate of Merck in Brazil.

> This strategy attacks a company's personal inflation rate at its source. Consider what a company has done when it has decided on its product mix. When it has decided what it will make, in what quantities, and by what process, it has determined its input inflation rate. When it had decided where it will market these products, at what price and in what quantities — so much locally and so much in non-local markets — it has determined its output inflation rate. In sum, it has fixed its corporate inflation rate.

Product mix changes are more likely to be applicable to manufacturers such as food, pharmaceuticals and chemicals, where a variety of products can be made on the same plant. The ability to change is restricted in industries such as brick-making, where the range of products which can be produced by the plant is limited.

Sufficient has been said in this and other chapters to indicate that a period of heavy inflation should be taken as a signal to re-examine investment decisions and research and development activity. The total economic justification for a planned expansion or line of research may have changed, or be about to change. Where possible the company would be advised to avoid investments in projects with a long lead time and heavy capital requirement, because in these the impact of inflation is less easy to control. This is advice that not all can follow, for not all companies are in situations where they have a real choice. In these circumstances the company might reduce its risks by reconsidering its policy on joint ventures and partnerships. Projects which can be divided into self-contained economic units would be preferable to ones which are all or nothing, for these at least provide the company with opportunities to restrict further investment if required. London Transport's Underground railways provide examples of such self-contained projects. The Victoria line was built in stages and the same approach has been adopted for the Fleet line. In the latter case, the full project has been postponed, although individual stages of the project are self-contained and are being completed.

Projects should also be considered against a multinational background for relative positions may have changed and competitive forces have altered.

Much of this chapter has been taken up with aspects of marketing strategy, and the implications which these have on investment and other decisions. Inflationary conditions also have an impact on administration and finance — indeed one might argue that there are no areas of the company which can escape this modern disease.

One of the major stumbling blocks to swift action in many companies is administrative procedures. Price increases are a complex exercise for many companies, in many cases involving a change of price lists, notification to customers and salesmen, and changing computer data so that invoices are issued at the appropriate rates. Only the customers and salesmen like price increases less than the administrative staff involved in making these changes. Where catalogues and sales literature are involved, price alterations may be expensive, unless the probability that they would occur was taken into account in the design of the material. When inflation runs high price increases will be frequent. The mechanism for making these changes must be overhauled, for there is nothing more frustrating than knowing that revenue is being lost because the company does not possess the ability to effect a speedy change to prices.

Parallel to this is the need to cope with more frequent changes to payrolls. Salary and wage rates are likely to be increased more frequently than the traditional annual review (see Chapter 9 for further discussion) and the company's systems must be geared to this.

The financial implications of severe inflation are that the company's need for cash is likely to be exceeded by the need of its customers, at least in their eyes. This suggests that the administrative procedures for debt collection should be re-examined, and the departments involved strengthened where necessary as they will have more work to do. Terms of business should be thoroughly reviewed, and if necessary rewritten to provide customers with an incentive to make prompt payment. Cash discounts may be unsuccessful, and a workable alternative might be to charge interest on overdue accounts. More care should be taken in deciding credit levels, for conditions of hyperinflation tend to increase the incidence of insolvency, either through pressure on profits or through the drying up of liquid funds. Credit control, always an important function, becomes even more vital.

Conversely the company should try to obtain as much trade credit as it can. In fact it will be well advised to do all the things it should be trying to check with its own customers, for this is a means of increasing liquidity at low rates of interest, the true price being the sacrifice of any prompt payment discount which might be offered. To operate such a policy, the company needs creditors who are less aggressive than it intends to be with its own customers. All other things being equal, better credit facilities (allowed or taken) might be a reason for changing suppliers.

A slow payment policy requires careful administration, partly to ensure that all debts are paid eventually, and partly to see that those which must be dealt with promptly are correctly isolated. It also needs a tactful contact staff, who can deal successfully with written and telephone requests for payment. The company may gain a reputation as a slow-payer: it must ensure that it never is charged with being a non-payer.

If all companies operate with equal efficiency no companies will be able to gain from a slow payment policy. In fact all businesses will never be equally effective, and those giving inadequate attention to these factors will be making an involuntary contribution to the profits of the more efficient operators. The worst position to be in is to pay all bills promptly — and allow all customers to take extended credit. Yet some companies will do just this.

Because cash flow will be under pressure, more attention should be given to financial planning and control. Monitoring and reporting procedures should be re-examined, including the frequency of review, and decisions made against assessments of the future rather than the pattern of the past.

The additional stresses of inflation call for each company to take a new look at all of its operations and procedures. It is the company which is most alive to the areas which must be changed which is most likely to survive any period of difficulty. Those that merely muddle on without thought are likely to suffer the most. Inflation can be a cruel tutor to those who are slow to learn.

Appendix 1: Formula for contract price adjustment in respect of variations in cost

Contract price adjustment for lifts

The prices quoted in this tender are based on costs current at the date of our tender.

If, by reason of any rise or fall in the cost of materials, labour or transport, or of conforming to any Act of Parliament or to any order, regulation, or bye-law made with statutory authority by Government Departments or by local or other authorities that shall be applicable to the works, above or below such costs ruling at the date of the tender, the cost to the Contractor of performing his obligations under the Contract shall be increased or reduced, the amount of such increase or reduction shall be added to or deducted from the Contract Price as the case may be, in accordance with the formula below.

Formula for calculating adjustments in respect of changes in cost of labour and materials.

A. *Wages*

(i) 47 per cent of the contract price shall be considered as works labour and adjusted by the percentage difference between the index figure for average earnings for Mechanical Engineering Workers issued by the Department of Employment last published before the date of Tender and the average of the index figures last published before the date of commencement of manufacture and date of completion of manufacture.

(ii) 23 per cent of the contract price shall be considered as erection labour and adjusted by the percentage difference between the index figure for average earnings for Electrical Engineering Workers issued by the Department of Employment last published before the date of Tender and the average of the index figures last published before the date of commencement of erection and date of completion of erection.

B. *Materials*
(i) 18 per cent of the contract price shall be adjusted in proportion to any fluctuation in the Department of Trade and Industry index figure for Materials used in the Mechanical Engineering Industry, between the date of tender and the start of the manufacturing period.
(ii) 12 per cent of the contract price shall be adjusted in proportion to any fluctuation in the Department of Trade and Industry index figure for Materials used in the Electrical Machinery Industry, between the date of tender and the start of the manufacturing period.

For the purpose of these calculations:
(i) The manufacturing period shall be taken as the last 3 months prior to completion of manufacture.
(ii) The index figures described above shall be adjusted to include a factor to take account of any increases, or decreases in respect of out-workers allowances, payments in respect of holidays, national insurance and other statutory payments, or the effects on any reduction in the working week.

The price will be subject to further variation in respect of any additional items arising by virtue of any statute, regulations or orders issued by any Government Departments or other duly constituted authority, and the Contractor shall be under no liability for non-fulfilment of any obligation to the extent that this is prevented, frustrated or impeded as a consequence of such statute, regulations or orders.

Note: Special consideration may be necessary in respect of imported equipments.

This formula will also be applied to those firm price contracts which exceed the firm price period. In such event, the formula would be applied to the uncompleted portion of the work as at the date of expiry of the firm price period.

Appendix 2: Price variation clauses of the standard contract of the Joint Contracts Tribunal

31A The Contract Sum shall be deemed to have been calculated in the manner set out below and shall be subject to adjustment in the events specified hereunder:

(*a*) (i) The prices (including the cost of employer's liability insurance and of third party insurance) contained in the Contract Bills are based upon the rates of wages and the other emoluments and expenses (including holiday credits) which will be payable by the Contractor to or in respect of workpeople engaged upon or in connection with the Works in accordance with the rules or decisions of the National Joint Council for the Building Industry and the terms of the Building and Civil Engineering Annual and Public Holidays Agreements which will be applicable to the Works and which have been promulgated at the date of tender, or in the case of workpeople so engaged whose rates of wages and other emoluments and expenses (including holiday credits) are governed by the rules or decisions or agreements of some body other than the National Joint Council for the Building Industry, in accordance with the rules or decisions or agreements of such other body which will be applicable and which have been promulgated as aforesaid.

(ii) If any of the said rates of wages or other emoluments and expenses (including holiday credits) are increased or decreased by reason of any alteration in the said rules, decisions or agreements promulgated after the date of tender, then the net amount of the increase or decrease in wages and other emoluments and expenses (including holiday credits) together with the net amount of any consequential increase or decrease in the cost of employers' liability insurance, of third party insurance and of any contribution, levy or tax payable by a person in his capacity as an employer, shall, as the case may be, be paid to or allowed by the Contractor.

(*b*) (i) The prices contained in the Contract Bills are based upon the types and rates of contribution, levy and tax payable by a person in his capacity as an employer and which at the date of tender are payable by the Contractor. A type and a rate so payable are in the next sub-paragraph referred to as a 'tender type' and a 'tender rate'.

(ii) If any of the tender rates other than a rate of levy payable by virtue of the Industrial Training Act 1964, is increased or decreased, or if a tender type ceases to be payable, or if a new type of contribution, levy or tax which is payable by a person in his capacity as an employer becomes payable after the date of tender, then in any such case the net amount of the difference between what the Contractor actually pays or will pay in respect of workpeople whilst they are engaged upon or in connection with the Works or because of his employment of such workpeople upon or in connection with the Works, and what he would have paid had the alteration, cessation or new type of contribution, levy or tax not become effective, shall, as the case may be, be paid to or allowed by the Contractor.

(iii) The prices contained in the Contract Bills are based upon the types and rates of refund of contributions, levies and taxes payable by a person in his capacity as an employer and upon the types and rates of premium receivable by a person in his capacity as an employer being in each case types and rates which at the date of tender are receivable by the Contractor. Such a type and such a rate are in the next sub-paragraph referred to as a 'tender type' and a 'tender rate'.

(iv) If any of the tender rates is increased or decreased or if a tender type ceases to be payable or if a new type of refund of any contribution levy or tax payable by a person in his capacity as an employer becomes receivable or if a new type of premium receivable by a person in his capacity as an employer becomes receivable after the date of tender, then in any such case the net amount of the difference between what the Contractor actually receives or will receive in respect of workpeople whilst they are engaged upon or in connection with the Works or because of his employment of such workpeople upon or in connection with the Works, and what he would have received had the alteration, cessation or new type of refund or premium not become effective, shall, as the case may be, be allowed by or paid to the Contractor.

(v) The references in the two preceding sub-paragraphs to premiums shall be construed as meaning all payments howsoever they are described which are made under or by virtue of an Act of Parliament to a person in his capacity as an employer and which affect the cost to an employer of having persons in his employment.

(vi) Where the Contractor elects to contribute to a recognised occupational pension scheme instead of participating in the Reserve Pension Scheme established under the Social Security Act 1973 the Contractor shall for the purpose of recovery or allowance under this clause be deemed to pay employer's contributions to the Reserve Pension Scheme.

(vii) The references in sub-paragraphs (i) to (iv) and (vi) of this paragraph to contributions, levies and taxes shall be construed as meaning all impositions payable by a person in his capacity as an employer howsoever they are described and whoever the recipient which are imposed under or by virtue of an Act of Parliament and which affect the cost to an employer of having persons in his employment.

(*c*) (i) The prices contained in the Contract Bills are based upon the market prices of the materials and goods specified in the list attached thereto which were current at the date of tender. Such prices are hereinafter referred to as 'basic prices', and the prices stated by the Contractor on the said list shall be deemed to be the basic prices of the specified materials and goods.

(ii) If after the date of tender the market price of any of the materials or goods specified as aforesaid increases or decreases, then the net amount of the difference between the basic price thereof and the market price payable by the Contractor and current when the materials or goods are bought shall, as the case may be, be paid to or allowed by the Contractor.

(iii) The references in the two preceding sub-paragraphs to 'market prices' shall be construed as including any duty or tax by whomsoever payable which is payable under or by virtue of any Act of Parliament on the import, purchase, sale, appropriation, processing or use of the materials or goods specified as aforesaid.*

31C (1) If the Contractor shall decide subject to clause 17 of these Conditions to sublet any portion of the Works he shall incorporate in the sub-contract provisions to the like effect as the provisions of clauses 31A and 31B which are applicable for the purposes of this Contract.

(2) If the price payable under such a sub-contract as aforesaid is decreased below or increased above the price in such sub-contract by reason of the operation of the said incorporated provisions, then the net amount of such decrease or increase shall, as the case may be, be allowed by or paid to the Contractor under this Contract.

31D (1) The Contractor shall give a written notice to the Architect of the occurrence of any of the events referred to in such of the following provisions as are applicable for the purpose of this Contract:

(*a*) Clause 31A(*a*) (ii);
(*b*) Clause 31A(*b*) (ii);
(*c*) Clause 31A(*b*) (iv);
(*d*) Clause 31A(*c*) (ii);
(*e*) Clause 31B(*a*) (ii);
(*f*) Clause 31B(*a*) (iv);
(*g*) Clause 31B(*b*) (ii);
(*h*) Clause 31C(2)

(2) Any notice required to be given by the preceding sub-clause shall be given within a reasonable time after the occurrence of that to which the notice relates, and the giving of a written notice in that time shall be a condition precedent to any payment being made to the Contractor in respect of the event in question.

(3) The Quantity Surveyor and the Contractor may agree what shall be deemed for all the purposes of this Contract to be the net amount payable to or allowable by the Contractor in respect of the occurrence of any event such as is referred to in any of the provisions listed in sub-clause (1) of this Condition.

* Clause 31B which is an alternative to 31A in certain circumstances has not been reproduced.

(4) Any amount which from time to time becomes payable to or allowable by the Contractor by virtue of clause 31A or clause 31B or clause 31C of these Conditions shall, as the case may be, be added to or subtracted from:

(*a*) The Contract Sum; and

(*b*) Any amounts payable to the Contractor and which are calculated in accordance with either sub-paragraph (i) or sub-paragraph (ii) of paragraph (b) of sub-clause 2 of clause 26 of these Conditions; and

(*c*) The amount which would otherwise be stated as due in the next Interim Certificate.

Provided:

(i) No addition to or subtraction from the amount which would otherwise be stated as due in an Interim Certificate shall be made by virtue of this sub-clause unless on or before the date as at which the total value of work, materials and goods is ascertained for the purposes of that Certificate the Contractor shall have actually paid or received the sum which is payable by or to him in consequence of the event in respect of which the payment or allowance arises.

(ii) No addition to or subtraction from the Contract Sum made by virtue of this sub-clause shall alter in any way the amount of profit of the Contractor included in that Sum.

(5) Clause 31A, clause 31B and clause 31C shall not apply in respect of:

(*a*) Work for which the contractor is allowed daywork rates under clause 11 (4) (*c*) (ii) of these Conditions.

(*b*) Work executed or materials or goods supplied by any nominated sub-contractor or nominated supplier (fluctuations in relation to nominated sub-contractors and nominated suppliers shall be dealt with under any provision in relation thereto which may be included in the appropriate sub-contract or contract of sale) or

(*c*) Work executed by the Contractor for which a tender made under clause 27(*g*) of these Conditions has been accepted.

(*d*) Changes in the rate of value added tax charged on the supply of goods or services by the Contractor to the Employer under this Contract.

(6) In clause 31A and clause 31B of these Conditions:

(*a*) The expression 'the date of tender' means the date 10 days before the date fixed for the receipt of tenders by the Employer; and

(*b*) The expressions 'materials' and 'goods' include timber used in formwork but do not include other consumable stores, plant and machinery.

(*c*) The expression 'workpeople' means persons whose rates of wages and other emoluments (including holiday credits) are governed by the rules or decisions or agreements of the National Joint Council for the Building Industry or some other like body for trades associated with the building industry.

References

BUILDING EDC (1974) 'Price adjustment formulae for building contracts', National Economics Development Office, p. 2.

LIETAER, B. A. (1970) 'Prepare your company for inflation', *Harvard Business Review*, September/October.

8

Purchasing

Raw materials and supplies have already been discussed several times in this book. Chapter 1 illustrates the broad impact of raw material inflation on strategic decisions, and Chapter 6 shows how indices may be created so that this aspect of inflation can be monitored.

Purchasing can only 'come right' if it is organised to cope with modern, inflationary conditions. Traditionally raw materials and supplies have rarely been a board room topic for industrial companies, and very few have considered the strategic implications of purchasing decisions. Although the professional buyer has long been a respected feature of the British management scene, he is too rarely of director level and seldom seen as a key element in a total logistics function. Frequently he is too much a buyer, and too little a manager.

No doubt 1974, with its twin themes of unpredicted shortages and rapidly rising prices, caused some upset of this tradition, and there cannot be a board room in the country which did not give more attention to procurement in this single year than in the whole of the preceding decade. This follows the normal top management custom of concentrating on the problem areas.

This sort of unexpected intrusion into top management's attention is the result of a failure to organise the purchasing function in the best way. Few companies have a forward plan for purchases, and usually little attention is given to forecasting raw material sources and prices. What is needed is an approach to the management of purchasing which regularly ensures that these things are properly investigated and considered. It has been estimated that the cost of raw materials, supplies and purchased services averages about 50 per cent of the final selling price of manufactured items. Averages are seldom typical, but this sort of order of magnitude suggests that few companies can afford to neglect purchasing in developing their anti-inflation policies. The whole area offers a potential source of profit opportunity.

Taylor (1974, p. 17) draws a parallel between purchasing and marketing. He suggests that the gradual acceptance of the marketing concept by consumer product companies led to a realisation that selling and marketing were not the same, and to the growth of marketing departments and the development and improvement of techniques such as marketing research. Levitt (1960, p. 39) coined the phrase 'marketing myopia' to describe the state which many were in at the start of this period. Now, Taylor argues, we have reached a state of 'purchasing myopia', when a purchasing concept should be developed which 'would in essence do for Buying what Marketing has done for selling: it has given business a new philosophy, or different view of strategy and a research and planning capability to cope with the threat'.

Davies (1974, p. 4) suggests an approach to purchasing management which divides the function into strategic (a horizon of three years and over), tactical (1—2 years) and operational (day to day). For the first he postulates a centralised purchase planning and research group, for the second centralised purchasing product managers, and for the third decentralised operational buyers. Under this concept the purchase planning and research group would be responsible for the preparation of a purchasing plan, the strategic interaction of purchasing with the rest of the company, the arranging of an information base and forecasting. Purchasing product managers would be experts on key raw materials on a worldwide basis, taking the long-term plan to a tactical level. Responsibility for buying all items at their particular location would remain with the operational buyers, although this would be in conjunction with the product managers when key raw materials are involved.

An alternative new approach to organising the purchasing activity is suggested by Lalonde and Robeson (1971). This is summarised in Fig. 8.1 and sees purchasing as part of a total logistics function. Under this concept forecasting also has a prominent place.

Perhaps either of these two approaches would be too big a change for many companies. A less revolutionary compromise might be to add a research and planning capability to the existing purchasing organisation, and at the same time to ensure that the corporate planning system allows the purchasing department to influence strategic decisions. In most companies there is a clear need for additional manpower and financial resources to be allocated to purchasing, for without this few purchasing departments have either the capacity or the skills to undertake the necessary research and analytical work.

The basic requirements from such a reshaped purchasing department lay considerable stress on forecasting and information. Most buyers in all organisations are involved in short-term price forecasting, and normally have an influence on the cost of supplies assumptions used in annual budgets and standard costs. Frequently this form of forecasting

Fig. 8.1 Purchasing as part of a total logistics function

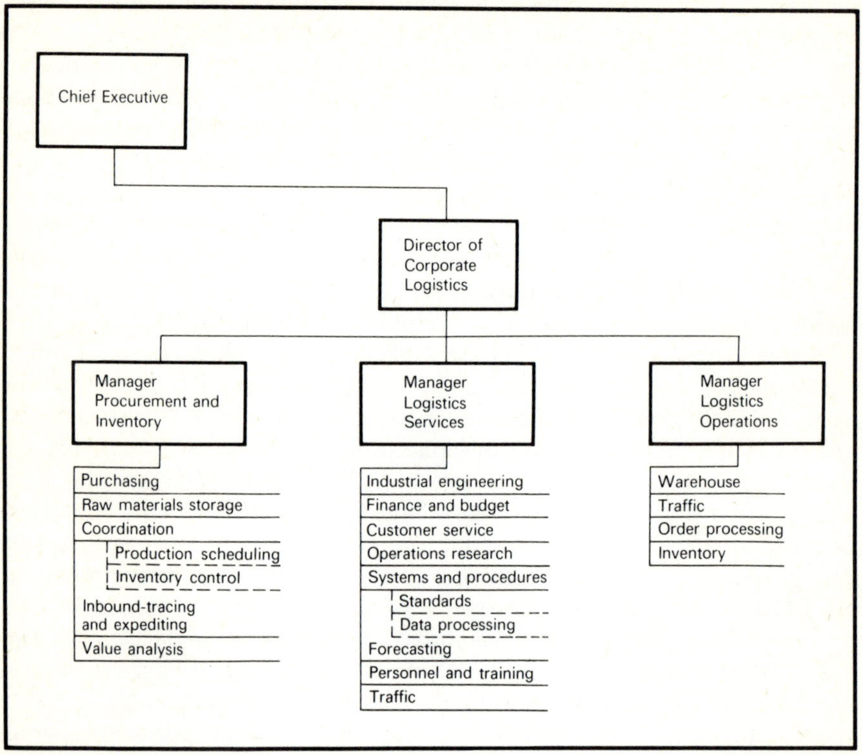

is based on a mixture of intuition and supplier contact rather than any form of scientific approach. In some ways these forecasts resemble those that can be collected by passing the hat round the sales force, and collating all the contributions dropped into it. The results are unlikely to be accurate, and at best can be used only for short-term decisions.

There are exceptions: buyers who specialise in particular commodities may develop a high level of expertise and awareness which cannot be bettered for short-term forecasts. The commodity buyer is, however, a feature of a comparatively small number of businesses, and in many of these the total purchasing requirement embraces numerous additional items.

Forecasting effort needs to be directed at the availability of raw materials and supplies, and price movements. It should provide data which can be used for both the short term and the long term, and should lead to better decisions. Improved short-term forecasts can enable better budgeting and control to take place: better long-term forecasts can give early warning of problems and opportunities, while the company still has time to change course to cope with them.

An improvement in forecasting depends partly on technique, partly on information, and much more on common sense and effort applied to the problem. Forecasting techniques have been well established in other fields and can be applied to the supply and demand situation, and the resultant price trends. Into this consideration should be brought the question of available substitutes. Much of what is needed is in fact a form of market forecast, seen from the viewpoint of purchasing. Kingsman (1974, p. 24) has suggested how operational research techniques can be used to help commodity buyers to achieve a better purchasing performance. There is every reason to believe that econometric models, which may be used with confidence for marketing forecasts, can also be developed for purchasing.

Forecasting is only a means to an end, and the most accurate of forecasts will never have more than academic value unless it influences decisions. This is why purchasing must be seen as an integrated part of the total corporate plan, and not as an isolated service department of production.

Information, that other criteria of better forecasts, rarely comes to hand regularly on an accidental basis. The collection of information requires organisation, evaluation and analysis, and is something with which many buying departments are inadequately supplied.

The purchasing department must generate internal information on the company's future supply requirements (which is a form of planning) and obtain external data on the markets of which the company's supplies may form only a small part. The first requirement is a dynamic exercise, related to purchasing and inventory policies and to marketing and production plans. It is dynamic because if planning is seriously undertaken the decisions which arise from the forecasts of how to meet these requirements may themselves change the specifications, volume or price of the products required.

A market research type capability is a requirement for the collection of external data. In effect, the purchase researcher has to study the market of which his purchases are an integral part and to carry this study further so that it covers the capacity and capability of the alternative suppliers to that market. The purchasing man has a big advantage over his marketing counterpart in that he can often obtain the active cooperation of suppliers in furtherance of his study.

Few purchasing research sections will ever be in a position to provide detailed information and forecasts on every type of product in the procurement programme. Concentration would normally be on the major items purchased or on specific problem areas. However, every product should have minimum information on alternative suppliers and their capability, and there should be a dossier on every supplier. Vendor knowledge should go further than a list of names and addresses, and should include a profile of the business, its management, financial performance, technical and delivery performance, capacity and the extent to which it is dependent for its survival on one or two major customers.

The information base should lead to two other steps in procurement planning: the revision of purchasing and inventory policies and a programme through which the supply requirement plan may be fulfilled. Policies are not immutable, and one of the functions of purchasing planning should be to assess the validity of old policies, and develop new ones where needed. The programme for supplies should include contingency measures and backup plans so that all that is humanly possible is done in advance to ensure future supplies. Throughout the year this part of the programme should be monitored and adjusted where necessary.

Forecasts are only inputs into plan. The need to improve forecasting ability comes directly from the need to make better decisions, many of which will go far wider than the traditional purchasing approach which is concerned mainly with continuity of supplies and price.

Taylor (1974, p. 21) has suggested an analytical approach to purchasing strategies which follows a similar line of thought to the product/market matrix shown in Fig. 5.3. The purchasing matrix, illustrated in Fig. 8.2, attempts to relate sources of supplies to alternative technologies, and may be used to help identification of some of the many possible courses of action which should arise from any future oriented study of purchasing strategy.

Fig. 8.2 Analysis of alternative supply strategies

Technology / Suppliers	Existing	New
Existing	Improve present technology/ Develop present suppliers	Develop substitute materials/ less wasteful technology
New	Develop new suppliers Explore new geographical sources	Diversify into new technology requiring new suppliers and new materials or no materials

Existing supplies/existing technology. One of the first questions that should be raised is whether the current components of the problem can be improved, which may mean attention to the suppliers, the technology, or both. Technology may be modified: examples are the use of improved insulation to reduce fuel consumption by cutting down heat loss; a modification of specifications and buying standard so that a cheaper but equally effective product is purchased; a deliberate attempt to reduce wastage. The wartime CC41 products demonstrated how the reduction of waste could be built into product design and specifications: for example a plain upholstery fabric will give less waste than one which requires extensive pattern-matching. Everyone who has done home decorating will know how the type of pattern affects the quantity of wallpaper needed.

Sometimes technology improvements may be made completely 'in house'. Equally possible is cooperative improvement in conjunction with existing suppliers. Possibly Marks and Spencer lead the world in the way in which they develop their suppliers — the practical assistance may go beyond simple cooperation and includes training in modern methods and techniques. This sort of development is a long way away from the stereotype of the tough buyer which extracts such stringent conditions and low prices out of his suppliers that they eventually become bankrupt! In their own interests, companies should ensure that they do all they can to help their suppliers to stay in business.

Supplier development can take a financial form, such as deposits paid to a steel stockholder to ensure a minimum level of supplies, or even backwards integration with an equity involvement with a major supplier.

New suppliers existing technology. Strategic consideration may indicate a clear need for additional sources of supply, either from within or without the country. The trend will be increasingly for suppliers to be sought on a worldwide basis. Those companies operating in a multinational environment should examine the merits of a multinational approach to procurement. Invariably this is more difficult than it sounds and may reinforce a need for both rationalisation and standardisation of products. Many of the older multinational companies have significant variations in what is apparently the same product, because of local modification which occurred as factories were established in different countries. It is probable that strategies devised under this heading will be as a direct result of the 'existing supplies' approach above, and the changes in policies which are likely after a complete review of the purchasing situation.

Existing suppliers/new technology. The company which has a good relationship with suppliers may find it possible to cooperate with them to develop substitute raw materials or less wasteful technology. The initiative for such developments may come from either the supplier or the purchaser. Cooperation may be either technical or financial, and can bring benefits to both parties. The supplier has a natural interest in retaining his customer, and ensuring a market for any new product he might develop. The buyer can obtain a level of technical support which might otherwise be difficult to achieve, and has the advantage of working with someone who has a good knowledge of his requirements and problem.

New suppliers/new technology. Despite the advantages suppliers might be expected to have in the development of new technology, it is more frequent for new approaches to come from quite different sources. Somehow the incentive for major innovation rarely springs from the person who has a profitable market for his present products. Purchasing strategies should seriously consider ways in which new technologies might be used, or identifying suppliers who would be willing to help to develop a material as a substitute for an existing substance which is running into a forecast shortage situation. The aim of purchasing planning is to enable the company to take the initiative to solve an anticipated problem, and thereby to avoid crises and expensive panic actions.

The framework provided by this matrix is only one way of looking at purchasing strategies and does not fully cover all the possibilities which should be considered. One of the most important additional areas for study is the interaction of the supply forecasts (price and volume), and the alternative supply strategies with other functions in the company: marketing, production and finance.

Perhaps the most obvious need is a dialogue with marketing to assess the impact of the purchasing forecasts of marketing strategy. Elsewhere it has been argued that the right answer under conditions of high inflation will rarely be to increase selling prices and expect volume to be unchanged. If the strategy is to increase prices, the product demand should be reassessed, which may in turn lead to a change in the expected raw material requirements.

Strategies may become more complicated when price changes are likely to bring an unacceptable market reaction, or will run contrary to anti-inflation legislation. In some circumstances the cost of supplies may not be as great an influencing factor as the difficulty of obtaining them at all! Nineteen-seventy-four was a year of raw material price escalation and world shortages. Forecasts made today suggest that there is a strong possibility that the future holds further periods when certain materials and supplies, including energy, will be difficult to obtain or may be subject to some form of rationing.

Although marketing might be completely satisfied that the product it offers meets all consumer requirements, the expectation of uncertainty of supplies and rising costs might provide a strong incentive to modify the product. Successful marketing is not just the provision of consumer satisfaction, but doing this in a way which meets the company's profit criteria.

One advantage of purchasing planning is that it can provide earlier warning of the need to make product changes in this type of circumstance. Adequate notice allows time for investigation and for market tests on the new product. Failure to consider such possibilities can result in panic actions which allow no opportunity for market study, or a decision to continue selling at a less than adequate contribution. In extreme cases there may be an unplanned (and possibly avoidable) withdrawal of the product from the market.

The planned approach rarely makes the problem go away, but it should give the company time to study its options and to ensure that the appropriate elements of marketing strategy are brought together in a way which helps the expected change along. If this does not mean a change to the product, or its price, it may mean re-examining promotional or distribution strategies, possibly suggesting a need to look again at growth strategies and the areas from which the company expects to obtain its future profits. The company may find that its entire conception of its present and future breadwinners changes as a result of the forecasts made in support of its purchasing plan.

Production strategies should also be considered in relation to the purchasing plan. At the simplest level, the consideration of supply forecasts in relation to costs and production methods might suggest a need to re-examine the standards set for purchased materials. This may, of course, take us back to item 1 of Fig. 8.2 and be developed in conjunction with suppliers. Value analysis techniques may also be useful, either alone or in association with suppliers.

More complex production decisions may arise when inflation expectations point to the need for a new process of manufacture. (Other elements of inflation, besides purchases, may also contribute to such a need.) New processes may be chosen because they reduce wastage, process a lower priced variant of the raw material, use less energy, or (and this is not related to the purchasing plan) reduce labour costs. Generally such changes require capital investment. Making such an investment to reduce future costs may be a valid alternative to the other possible marketing strategies, and enable the company to hold prices and gain a competitive advantage which may help it to gain volume at the expense of its rivals.

Major changes foreshadowed in the purchasing plan may therefore lead to a complete re-examination of the economics of production and the approach to marketing. But this is not all, for the purchasing plan will also have financial implications which cannot be ignored.

Consequential implications, arising from a new capital investment or a changed marketing strategy are fairly obvious and are unlikely to be overlooked. Even without any such decisions, the purchasing plan has an impact on finance, through its approach to inventories. Cash flows may be affected in numerous different circumstances which arise either from inflation of the cost of supplies, or from expected shortages. Cost increase may lead to higher inventory levels even where inventory policies are unchanged and expected purchase volumes are unaffected. This inflation of inventory values will certainly change cash flow needs, and may reduce profits by creating an additional interest burden.

Far more likely is that the purchasing plan will lead to a change in purchasing behaviour. It may, for example, be considered strategically necessary to hold a higher volume of inventories as a reserve against probable supply problems. This may mean an increase in financial requirements far above the forecast rate of cost inflation. In extreme cases the company may not be able to support the sort of purchasing policy which now appears to be so important. Once again the benefit of purchasing planning is that it provides the company with time to evaluate, decide and organise. A cash flow problem which can be accurately forecast some time ahead is more likely to be solved than one which arrives as an unexpected event.

Risk, sensitivity analysis and alternative planning assumptions were discussed in Chapter 5. It is perhaps unnecessary to add to this chapter, except to urge that the same concepts be applied both to purchasing plans and to strategies resulting from considering the implications of purchasing price and source forecasts on corporate decisions. In many cases a study of risk and sensitivity will help the company to choose the best course of action from those available to it.

It might be revolutionary thinking for suggested acquisition strategies, or proposals for new activities such as the recycling of waste materials, to emerge from the purchasing section. Although these will have an essentially supply orientation, they may well lead to new marketing activities for the company. A recycling project could, for example, process waste from other sources and might produce raw materials for sale as well as for further processing. Backwards integration to secure supply lines might involve the purchase of a company with a marketing commitment to other customers.

What is needed is an imaginative approach to procurement, a better understanding of supply sources and trends, and a commitment to fighting inflation from the buying side of the company. As has been shown, winning this battle need not be an attempt to push vendors' prices down to uneconomic levels (which could indeed work against the long-term interests of the company) and could well be the result of changing the battlefield. Sometimes the battle will be won by basically changing raw material requirements; on other occasions the answer might lie in closer cooperation with suppliers. Whatever the solution, it will only come about in those companies which organise their purchasing activity so that it can play a meaningful role in the future of the company, and for most companies this means a great deal of thought and a changed attitude to procurement.

References

DAVIES, O. (1974) 'The marketing approach to purchasing management', *Long Range Planning*, 7, no. 3, p. 4.

KINGSMAN, B. G. (1974) 'Forecasting and research for supply markets — commodity buying systems', *Long Range Planning*, 7, no. 5, p. 24.

LALONDE, B. J. and ROBESON, J. F. (1971) 'Corporate strategy and organisation for distribution', *Long Range Planning*, 2, no. 3.

LEVITT, T. (1960) 'Marketing myopia', *Harvard Business Review*, July—Aug.; reprinted in *Innovation in Marketing*, Pan, 1968, p. 39.

TAYLOR, B. (1974) 'Strategic planning for resources', *Long Range Planning*, 7, no. 4, p. 17.

9

Industrial relations and manpower

Industrial relations appeared briefly in Chapter 3, as one aspect of the effect on society of high rates of inflation. The treatment there was short and uncomplicated, and the subject now needs to be taken much further.

Industrial relations are affected by numerous external pressures of which inflation is but one. Even without hyperinflation industrial relations, in the UK at least, had reached a very poor state. This undoubtedly has had an effect on Britain's competitive performance in the world economy. Ball (1974, p. 197) observes:

> An underlying factor in Britain's failure to compete effectively has been its unsatisfactory industrial relations. For a combination of historical and sociological reasons, British workers give first loyalty to their unions rather than to the companies they work for. Within the British trade-union movement (Europe's strongest in terms of membership), authority is widely dispersed. Craft unions have persisted in Britain to an unusual degree, creating fragmentation of authority and responsibility on the shop floor and proliferation of 'demarcation disputes' about who does what.

An industrial relations climate is difficult to measure. Only one facet is illustrated by strikes (see Table 9.1), since industrial relations may be poor even when there are few strikes. Sanctions such as 'go-slows', 'working to rule', 'overtime bans', or 'working without enthusiasm' do not appear in the strike tables, nor does the productive time of managers and shop stewards which is lost in endless discussions and disputes. Loss of productivity through lack of motivation is a real thing which can rarely be demonstrated through statistical tables, partly because nobody knows what productivity really is. Even with these omissions the table demonstrates an alarming situation which can please no one.

Table 9.1 Industrial disputes — United Kingdom: working days lost in stoppages

Year	*All services and industry*	*Mining and quarrying*	*Metals, engineering, shipbuilding and vehicles*	*Textiles clothing and footwear*	*Construction*	*Transport and communications*	*All other*	*Total number of disputes*
1960	3,024	495	1,450	25	110	636	308	2,832
1961	3,046	740	1,464	22	285	230	305	2,686
1962	5,798	308	4,559	37	222	431	241	2,449
1963	1,755	326	854	25	356	72	122	2,068
1964	2,277	309	1,338	34	125	312	160	2,524
1965	2,925	413	1,763	52	135	305	257	2,354
1966	2,398	118	871	12	145	1,069	183	1,937
1967	2,787	108	1,422	31	201	823	202	2,116
1968	4,690	57	3,363	40	233	559	438	2,378
1969	6,846	1,041	3,739	140	278	786	862	3,116
1970	10,980	1,092	4,540	384	242	1,313	3,409	3,906
1971	13,551	65	6,035	71	255	6,539	586	2,228
1972	23,909	10,800	6,636	274	4,188	876	1,135	2,497
1973	7,197	91	4,799	193	176	331	1,608	2,873
1974	14,740	5,627	5,883	247	253	695	2,035	2,882

Source: Department of Employment Gazette.

Brown (1973, p. 7) states:

> Nevertheless there is currently a general feeling of pessimism about the employment situation. People say that employment is a rat race and will continue to be a rat race; that advancing technology will condemn more and more people to deadening boredom or worse, unemployment; that the gap between management and labour is inevitable; and that the highest rewards will go to the slick or the bellicose.

In fairness it should be stressed that Brown's contribution does not reflect the feeling of pessimism he describes. His views will be discussed later.

Periods of high inflation tend to increase the standing of trade unions, because of the large settlements they are able to negotiate. A 20 per cent increase sounds impressive and much better than 5 per cent: it is easy to forget that the real value of either is related to inflation of prices and the purchasing power of money.

Brown (1973, p. 78) makes another pertinent comment which explains part of the cause of the vicious spiral of large increases which begins once one group of workers gains ground.

> The demands for increased wages are largely based, not on the absolute value of what is sought, but on acute anxiety on the part of occupational groups that they are falling behind others in the race.
>
> All of us, as employees, are being forced, by the current situation, to defend the standard of living of our families by joining with others in the use of power. We have in recent years been forced to accept that if we are reasonable we are left behind in the differential wage race whereas militancy brings home the lolly. If we fail to combine for strength then we are left with the burden of paying, out of relatively low wages, the higher prices for everything brought about by the high wage deals forced through by others.

Steep rises in the prices of goods in the shops bring demands for wage increases. These are reinforced by press and television reports of large settlements made to other groups of workers — partly because of the anxiety mentioned by Brown, and partly because the settlements demonstrate that some employers at least are willing to pay more. Flushed with apparently large successes, and backed by the genuine fears and anxieties of its members, each union becomes more militant in its demands.

The problem of relativities has become painfully acute in recent years, not only the relationship one group of skilled operatives has with another in the same company, industry or economy at large, but also in the disappearing differentials between clerical and manual workers, between supervisors and the men they manage. Here is fertile ground for the white-collar militancy referred to in Chapter 3. It is not surprising that staff and professional unions are increasing in strength, nor that one now hears talk of the justification of a 'third force' of senior managers and professional men to act as a counterbalance to the power of the unions.

The traditional pattern of annual reviews of staff salaries and once a year increases for hourly paid men is being challenged. Indeed it is questionable whether annual agreements between unions and employers have ever been very firm, and disputes frequently break out before the term of agreement has expired. On the staff side it is normal in many companies for the annual review to adjust salaries for inflation over the previous twelve months and to pay an additional element for 'merit' where justified. The inflation rate for the preceding period also plays a part in negotiations with other groups of workers.

This approach works very well when inflation is around 5 to 8 per cent. Inflation of 20 per cent is a different question and under these conditions employees are unwilling to wait twelve months; they require either some form of interim payment or some attempt to anticipate future inflation. In 1974 a form of indexation, threshold payments, was given the seal of Government approval as part of the anti-inflation legislation. In the same year the TUC negotiated the mystical 'social contract' which purported to restrict wage increases to past inflation.

The National Institute of Economics and Social Research (1974) observes:

> However, this rule — of compensation for past price increases only — is not being followed. Such compensation has already been given by the stage 3 thresholds, but many current settlements are for increases of the order of 20 per cent, *in anticipation* of further price rises of this order in the coming twelve months. 20 per cent inflation thus becomes a self-fulfilling prophecy. Through the mechanism of relativity comparisons, settlements of this order may now spread extensively through the labour force.

The danger of salaries going out of control is increased because salary survey data quickly lose validity in conditions of high inflation. In more stable days the annual surveys carried out by many commercial organisations gave a fair measure of guidance on the competitiveness of the company's salary policies. When increases are given more frequently than once a year, even the most up-to-date surveys face the danger of reporting a past which gives no guide to the present. This makes it harder for companies to be sure that their salary policies are fair to employees and therefore makes them less well equipped to deal with interim salary claims.

In July 1975 the British Government once again introduced a system of statutory wage control, accepting that the 'social contract' had failed. Experience of previous attempts at legislative control suggest that this is essentially a temporary remedy, and that organisations should give thought to their longer term wage policies on the assumption that inflationary conditions are likely to continue into the foreseeable future.

It is my opinion that few companies will be able to maintain an annual review of staff salaries, or a yearly agreement with other workers, unless they are accompanied by index-linked rises, threshold payments or some other mechanism for ensuring that cost of living rises are met by wage increases. Conceding this at an early stage can avoid a great deal of spasmodic industrial action later. The growing militancy of all employees, backed by their genuine fears of losing the race against inflation and other groups of workers, is enough to make industrial action inevitable when no mechanism is provided for inflation-linked increases.

One of the side effects of indexation systems or thresholds is that they make budgeting more difficult. Instead of one increase per year, the company now has to pay many, and must attempt to forecast not only the rates of increase but the dates of their occurrence. The only thing that can be said is that difficult though it may be, it is far easier to make budgeting calculations which are linked to an agreed formula, than to predict the random increases which will be inevitable in those companies which try to fight against indexation or thresholds.

A period of high inflation is, for the reasons discussed, likely to be a period of large wage concessions by employers. Despite the expected militancy of unions, it is a period when companies should deliberately set out to win concessions which lead to improved productivity. Ball (1974, p. 300) gives one view of British industrial relations problems.

> To remain in the same league with other industrialised countries, Britain will have to move from being a low-wage, low-productivity, low-investment society to being a high-wage, high-productivity, high-investment society. This shift, which clearly cannot be either quick or painless, will require contributions from labor — more shop floor discipline, more willingness to accept increased industrial efficiency. But it will also require contributions from management, including a bolder and more positive attitude toward capital investment, as well as more recognition that paying higher wages for increased productivity can be a good deal for both sides.

Increased productivity is a fine concept, and was behind an explosion of 'productivity bargaining' and payment by results schemes during the 1960s; an explosion which was assisted by Government action through the Prices and Incomes Board. One of the major difficulties is fundamental: the virtual impossibility of measuring productivity improvement, or, when it can be measured, to relate this to individual effort.

Because of these and other reasons these attempts to improve productivity have not proved to be the universal panacea which was expected. Perhaps the secret of the other reasons for failure lies in the fact that motivation by carrot is not very far advanced from motivation by stick, and recent developments in industrial psychology have demonstrated that human responses are much more complex than these simplistic approaches would suggest.

Where positive productivity improvements can be achieved through bargaining is, in my opinion, through the demolition of constraints rather than through payments linked to increased output. The abandonment of restrictive practices, willingness to accept new methods and flexibility are but three of the many areas where the constraints against productivity improvement are very strong. The three-day week in the UK during the first part of 1974 demonstrated clearly that where management and workers can combine in a common cause real improvements in output result. Corina (1968, p. 5), long before the three-day week, stated:

> Most of the evidence indicates that managements, throughout O.E.C.D. countries, will have to re-evaluate payment by results systems on a large scale. But productivity stimulation, as the evidence also suggests, can only be derived from a genuine collaborative effort. Throughout the work force, men have potentials and ideas about improvements, and they have the power either to enhance or frustrate the effectiveness of the organisation.

The problem remains what it always was: how to obtain this genuine collaborative effort — preferably without indulging in another three-day week! The dimensions of the problem are identified by two observations made nearly twenty years apart. Ling (1954, p. 9) wrote:

> In the countryside around any big city in England early on a Sunday morning one can see young men pedalling bicycles in amateur long-distance races with an enthusiasm that has to be seen to be believed. Sweat drips from their brows, their girlfriends have turned out to support them, other amateurs measure the time with stop watches and the bicyclists themselves appear keen and alive. These same people at their jobs in the factory look, feel and behave differently. They will often appear bored, irritated, frustrated and tense, probably grumbling about the management and perhaps watching the clock until they can leave. Some will be political extremists, others just the rather unhappy people who are to be found in every industrial community.
>
> In the first named situation they earn no money for their hard work on their bicycles but appear happy and cooperative. On the second they draw good wages at the end of the week but are often

> unhappy in the process. In the first named situation everyone will turn up if they can possibly manage it; in the factory escape into strikes, absenteeism, illness and psychosomatic breakdown is unduly common. Why the great difference?

Neal (1971, p. 168) makes a statement which suggests that only the bicycles have changed, the underlying attitudes being the same.

> Yet these same people, who bring so little enthusiasm to the work that provides them and their families with the standards of life, can, in other circumstances, apply themselves enthusiastically to the most unrewarding tasks. People will work without pay in Trade Union Branches, political parties, youth clubs, church activities. They diligently fling themselves under decaying old motor cars on Saturday mornings, while on Sunday they cultivate gardens and allotments to produce the most expensive vegetables you can imagine. When not engaged in these tasks, they are either eagerly watching dangerous football matches in appalling weather conditions, or, sitting for endless hours in the cold and damp by depressing rivers and canals fishing for unenthusiastic and inedible fish.
>
> What then is the explanation of this paradox? And perhaps more important, what is the solution?

This problem has been of critical importance for the UK for a long time, and has received the attention of managers, civil servants, consultants and academics without a great deal of success. Perhaps the worsening of industrial relations in the UK is evidence that industry has failed to identify and apply the appropriate solution.

Hyperinflation makes the problem hypercritical. First, because it is a period of acute difficulty for business, bringing with it an increased probability of failure and bankruptcy. Second, one way to combat inflation is to counter attack through lower costs, and many potential productivity gains require the cooperation and enthusiasm of the work force. Third, if inflation leads to increased militancy, this can easily extend from pay to demands for unproductive forms of participation or public ownership. Thus what is at stake is not only the continual existence of the company, but the UK's competitive position in the world economy, and the future shape of our industrial society and political organisation.

I believe the solution lies in a determined effort to apply the principles of the newer behavioural scientists; by seeking to explain why men work, these demonstrate concepts which can be used as motivation to work. Those who wish to refer in more detail to these developments are recommended to read Thomas and Bennis (1972) and Vroom and Deci (1970). It is easy to draw attention to some of the main contributors to the new thinking — McGregor, Likert, Herzberg, and Blake, but difficult to do more than give an impression of the underlying message in a book which must concentrate its efforts on its main theme — inflation.

In a nutshell, the concepts draw attention to the fact that man is a complex being, a 'wanting animal'. His needs are never satisfied. If he is short of the basic necessities of life his main motivation will be to obtain them. In these conditions, as in nineteenth-century Britain and certain overseas countries today, 'carrot and stick' principles will work. Once the basic necessities of life are provided for with a reasonable degree of certainty (and in a welfare state, no one need starve) man's needs change, and reach the higher levels which relate to his interaction with society (belonging, friendship) and finally shift to the ego-centred needs (for self-esteem, recognition, sense of achievement).

Further, it is apparent that much of our industrial organisation is based on the assumption that man is inherently lazy, and will only work if closely supervised. In fact it is possible to organise on an alternative assumption that quite the opposite applies. Bound up with this are questions of leadership style, and reasonable proof that methods which are based on distrust, tight control and 'carrot and stick' techniques are less effective than those which are less autocratic and which allow more personal freedom to contribute.

Most organisations create jobs and a working environment which frustrate man's higher needs, jobs which allow no pride of craftsmanship or sense of achievement, no opportunity to contribute his ideas to the way things are done and force him to work in acute boredom in what to him is a vacuum; he may have no concept of the aims and tasks of the organisation.

What is required is a close look at the nature of the jobs we ask people to do, the way in which these are organised and supervised and the mechanism's of control. Theories of job enrichment suggest that jobs can be redesigned so that they become more interesting and more exciting, and these concepts have been applied to one of the most monotonous of all mass production industries, motor vehicles. The Swedish Volvo company has redesigned its total production approach in order to provide more work satisfaction for individuals. In Britain the car industry offers high wages as the universal cure, and is currently right at the top as one of the most disrupted and dispute-ridden industries of them all.

With more satisfying jobs it should be possible to depart from the traditional approach to supervision to one that leans more to McGregor's theory Y: that men are not inherently lazy and will do an honest day's work. When a man is proud of his work, it becomes possible to allow him to exercise more self-control, to measure his performance and correct for failure because he wants to do his job well.

In my opinion these two states can only come about if there is a third: mutual trust and respect. Across much of British industry this is a non-existent commodity. Both 'management' and 'workers' expect to be cheated. From the management's point of view, the men are often intractable, inflexible and uncooperative. In their turn the men often see management as exploiters who are intractable, inflexible and uncooperative. To bridge this gap there must be participation from both sides. To achieve this requires an old fashioned concept — leadership.

It also requires a corresponding effort from trade unions, for a one-sided attempt to solve the many problems which beset British industrial relations will fail. The leadership to solve the problem should come from management for if it forfeits its right to lead through lack of action, management can only blame itself if the solutions which finally emerge are hostile to its interests.

Brown (1973, p. 79) suggests a solution to the wages conflict which would remove wage fixing from the purview of management. He maintains that three methods of controlling wages have failed: productivity based schemes, Government imposed limits or controls and arbitration by outside experts. The only realistic way to curb wage inflation and counteract the strength of large unions is to create a National Council for the Regulation of Differential Wages (NCRD). All employee categories would form unions which would elect the membership of the NCRD. Each year Parliament would hold an economic debate during which the allowable amount of increase of the national wage and salary bill would be fixed. Within this overall limit the NCRD would recommend to Government the increases which should be allowed for different groups of employees. Of course he has much more to say about how such a system might work, and his reasons for suggesting it. Perhaps most pertinent is his view that employers should play no part in this rate-fixing:

> The effect of excluding them and leaving the argument to be conducted between Trade Unions is to introduce the necessary countervailing power to that of individual Trade Unions. They are brought face to face with each other and must be placed in a situation where, within limits set by Parliament, they have to agree on how differential wages of the various sectors of employment shall be adjusted (p. 83).

Whether this constitutional solution to a situation hitherto considered an essential part of management decision making would work is a matter of conjecture, since no one has tried it.

Political and Economic Planning (PEP) (1973) argues that such a single national body would be unworkable, and that the solution to the earnings problem lies in an approach to national job evaluation. The report observes: 'Large sectors of British industry are still without systematic job evaluation schemes, still have decayed systems of payments by results and still operate manufactured overtime. An important factor then of any measures to establish greater general fairness in pay must be to ensure the reform of payments systems' (p. 38). The reasons offered in support of this suggested need are 'felt-fairness' over relativities, the fact that in company experience of job evaluation would bring greater confidence in a national scheme and the belief that the existence of national schemes of payment makes it easier for businesses to adhere to a national system of wage control.

PEP suggests a national body should be created which would encourage the reform of payment systems and the use of job evaluation within companies. Such encouragement would be partly through educational/consulting services and partly through structure: only companies with effective systems would be allowed to give real increases to employees.

Its second role would be to evaluate claims on a national or regional basis against its own benchmark evaluations of jobs representing different types of work common to many industries. It would also develop its own system of job evaluation for different types of work. This work, PEP argues, would enable it to identify pattern of differentials between industries on strictly comparable data. Thus giving it the information needed to guide the level of increase which should be allowed each industry. Distribution within the industry would be through its local evaluation schemes. The body would be given the power to impose sanctions on those who opposed its policies. The function of the body presupposes the existence of a control incomes policy. PEP (1974, p. 7) argues:

> To secure support for incomes policy is a major political enterprise which deserves a very high political priority because it is the alternative to a distasteful and dangerous policy of high unemployment. The merit of the social contract, even in its present limited form, is that it accords such a priority to securing Union support.
>
> The government must maintain that support in any future development of the social contract, but it must at the same time extend participation in the social contract to the employers and secure the widest possible support for the stabilisation and development programme among the public at large. . . .
>
> To devise a programme comprehensive enough to receive sufficiently solid support is, indeed, a major political task which will take some time.

Whether any of the postulated solutions are implemented, or would be effective, is a matter of opinion. The important fact is that inflation, together with the current social climate, is bringing incomes in particular and industrial relations in general to a stage where employers can expect many more outside influences — which may be given the force of law — on their freedom of action in solving the problems in their own way. This is no excuse for opting out, because the less attention business gives to finding its own solutions, the less influence it will have on the national situation. So the challenge here, as in other areas is to avoid using inflation as an excuse for failure to manage. Managers who do not manage have no other useful function.

References

BALL, R. (1974) 'Is the English sickness curable?', *Fortune*, May.

BROWN, W. (1973) *The Earnings Conflict*, Penguin Books (Pelican).

CORINA, J. (1968) 'Pay and productivity', *Industrial Society*, July.

LING, T. M. (ed.) (1954) 'Major psycho—social problems in industry', *Mental Health and Human Relations in Industry*, Lewis, p. 9.

NATIONAL INSTITUTE OF ECONOMIC AND SOCIAL RESEARCH (1974) 'Summary and appraisal', *Economic Review*, November, p. 4.

NEAL, L. F. (1971) 'Future trends in industrial relations', *Occupational Psychology*, 45, p. 168.

POLITICAL AND ECONOMIC PLANNING (1974) 'Incomes policy, differentials and social justice', in *Reshaping Britain: a programme of economic and social reform*, PEP, The Social Science Institute, pp. 31—49.

THOMAS, J. M. and BENNIS, W. G. (eds) (1972) *Management of Change and Conflict*, Penguin.

VROOM, V. M. and DECI, E. L. (eds) (1970) *Management and Motivation*, Penguin.

10

Cost reduction

The need for monitoring cost movements was discussed in Chapter 6; Chapter 8 gave attention to one major area of costs: raw materials and supplies. The purpose of this chapter is to examine costs from a broader front. Few managers would disagree that a major part of their jobs is about efficiency — about doing things which increase productivity either through reduced costs or because they bring improved profit flows to the company. Indeed, management has always been partly about efficiency in the production of goods or services. Most companies will also subscribe to one or more functions dedicated to improvement: general consultancy; works and methods study; systems analysis; organisation and method; value engineering; and a number of others.

At first sight it may seem superfluous to argue that one of the ways to combat inflation is to reduce costs, because this is exactly what many managers think they have been doing during their normal duties. Few would disagree with the argument, although some might be tempted to retort that the fact that a statement is true does not necessarily mean that it is helpful.

This sort of 'so what?' response is not as well justified as might at first appear. There are in fact two positive sides to the argument which are constructive and meaningful.

Cost reduction can either be a policy to cut back expense in line with changes in revenue, or it can be an important positive strategy to mitigate inflation by finding cheaper ways of doing things. The first aspect may be forced on a company, where inflation causes revenue to decline drastically, or where the Government is trying to 'cure' inflation by recession. In these circumstances productive employees may be laid off, and overheads slashed by draconian edicts which consider only the present and pay little regard to the future shape of the company. Sometimes companies have no option but to act in this manner; many are pushed into a state of panic and act in haste. Where this type of cost reduction becomes necessary it is always the better for thought and planning.

Although the above approach to cost reduction may be the result of inflation, it is the other aspect which is really the subject of this chapter, an aspect which may perhaps be better termed profit improvement, since part of its intentions is to stimulate change in a way that may affect revenue as well as costs. In an inflationary situation such improvements may mitigate the effects of severe cost increases, or may do even better and increase margins despite inflation.

There can be no organisation anywhere in the world, however efficient, which cannot improve its efficiency in some way. No matter how good its managers, no matter how seriously they take their duty to increase productivity, there is always something that can be done better. The only problems are what, how, and the difficulty of implementation.

Despite this fact, many managements believe they give adequate attention to profit improvement, and that there is nothing further they should do. There is enough case evidence in management literature to demonstrate the error of this belief. That dramatic improvement is possible is best illustrated by Dudley (1974), in his summary of studies carried out by the Department of Engineering Production in the University of Birmingham, including a major comparative productivity analysis of forty companies over the years 1968—72, and a series of case studies in forty-five companies, 1970—74. The findings of these studies indicate:

1. that in medium sized batch production factories (200—3,500 employees) in engineering and metalworking, no more than 20 per cent of the time taken to progress materials through a factory is spent productively and that — after allowing for time actually spent in transporting materials and in waiting for the completion of the batch — at least 70 per cent of throughput time is wholly non-productive;
2. that in these factories over the period 1968—72 neither labour nor plant was engaged on directly productive work for more than an average 50 per cent of the time available. In the case of both labour and machine utilisation the range between firms within an industry (varying from 20 to 70 per cent approximately) was very much greater than the averages for the four industrial groups studied, namely, electrical, iron and steel, nonferrous metals and motor vehicle components;
3. that in all the firms studied there was considerable scope for the more economical use of materials. For some, materials utilisation was as low as 30 per cent;
4. that it is quite common to find that the machines being used for

various manufacturing processes are of much greater capacity than is required for actual operations they are regularly required to perform;
5. that, in studies of machinery conditions, less than 25 per cent of all lathes studied were being run at speeds approximating to optimum (economic) cutting conditions. Similar findings were recorded for milling and grinding machines;
6. that the applications of modern production planning and control techniques, cost control, low cost automation and plant maintenance, within a company, are highly correlated with each other and with productive efficiency levels as indicated by a range of indices (e.g. earnings : cost, profit : cost, facilities utilisation, materials utilisation).

Dudley also maintains that 'a further point that has emerged from these studies is that increased productivity is not a primary objective of industrial companies'. It appears that many of the companies in this study could completely cancel out the effects of inflation for at least a year by improving efficiency. In broad terms, they could keep prices down and gain business at the expense of competitors, or raise prices with the market and take the additional profit, or employ a combination of these two actions.

The optimum price strategy can only be determined in the light of the unique circumstances of each company. The important factor is that profit improvement measures can bring flexibility. This is always important, and never more so than when the company is facing difficult circumstances. And difficult circumstances are frequently brought by severe inflation.

The argument for taking positive steps to improve profits, increase productivity, reduce costs (or whatever other term is chosen to describe this type of management action) is very strong. Certainly they are strong enough to suggest that even the most efficient of companies should review what it is doing in this area. A review may take the form of putting traditional profit improvement functions under the top management microscope, requesting operational managers to prepare detailed improvement plans for the areas under their control, or setting up some form of permanent or semipermanent approach to profit improvement. The last approach is to be preferred as it provides a better opportunity for the company to manage profit improvement.

One of the problems of the traditional profit improvement functions is that they tend to be self-contained, and work only within their own disciplines and activity areas. For many improvements this may be the appropriate approach. However it does tend to follow the philosophy that if a business is the sum of its parts, what is good for one of the parts must be good for the whole.

Unfortunately this is not always true. Businesses are really a series of systems and subsystems, which do not necessarily coincide with the traditional organisation chart. Work tends to be organised by function: systems flow across, linking numerous functions. Thus a change in one of the components of a system may not necessarily be to the benefit of the total system; at the same time a study of the whole can bring improvements which would not be realised by an examination of the individual parts in isolation.

Perhaps one of the most striking modern examples of this systems approach to management lies in physical distribution. A significant number of companies have reduced expenses in what for many is a high-cost area, by applying a total physical distribution concept to the organisation of this vital area. Traditionally the elements of distribution have tended to be split, both organisationally and as cost centres. Typically, packing and transport are adjuncts to production, packaging mainly a marketing decision area, warehousing may fall under either marketing or production, inventories under production or finance, and order processing and shipping documentation under administration or accounts. Decisions will be taken according to organisational responsibility. Management information may be organised in the same way, so that the total distribution costs may neither be stated nor be readily ascertainable.

Organisation under the total physical distribution concept changes the traditional structure and enables decisions to be taken on a systems approach. Thus an evaluation of air versus road transport would take into account factors other than the direct transport rate. For example, packing, warehousing and inventory levels could all be altered by a switch from one mode to the other. What decreases costs for one function can increase them for others and an analysis made on a partial basis can lead to the wrong decision.

The best example I know of improvements arising from a complete change in distribution methods is the world banana industry. Until recent years bananas were shipped on the stem, wrapped in sacking or plastic, from the growing countries. These ungainly bundles were difficult to handle by mechanical means. On arrival in the importing country the bananas were ripened on the stem in warehouses, and when ripe were cut into hands and packed in returnable wooden boxes for delivery to retailers. Now they are cut green from the stem in the producing country and packed into cartons. The fruit stays in these cartons during ripening and is delivered in the same cartons to the retailer. The cost advantages of the change were the ability to handle boxes mechanically, a reduction in warehouse labour in the receiving country, an increase in capacity of all ships and warehouses (partly because waste is no longer shipped, and partly because cartons of standard sizes can be stacked so that more fruit goes into a given space), and the problem of waste disposal in the receiving, usually urbanised, country was avoided.

It is interesting to note that many now regard physical distribution as a subsystem of a much larger logistics system, which also embraces materials management. This concept appeared briefly in Chapter 8.

These examples are given because they show clearly that there are situations where a corporate approach gives the best answer. There are at least three ways in which the company might achieve this:

- initiate control and coordinate profit improvement through a senior management committee;
- appoint a profit improvement manager with this function;
- attempt one of the planned, participatory approaches to profit improvement.

For those companies where committees are a way of management the first approach may be acceptable. My own feeling is that committees are rarely adequate for this sort of work, unless they are supported by people of the right calibre to do most of the initiation and investigatory work, and to ensure implementation of decisions. Committee can very easily become boring sessions of much talk and little action. To achieve effective profit improvement there must be a great deal of action. This is not to argue that the judicious use of committees may not be beneficial — indeed they appear in some of the participatory schemes.

The second course of action has been taken by a number of companies, and it is by no means uncommon to come across executives bearing the title Profit Improvement Manager. He is likely to be a senior man, of high calibre, probably reporting direct to the Managing Director. The reasons behind his appointment will include:

- the need to take a corporate view of profit improvement;
- the stimulation of other managers to take part in a profit improvement programme;
- initiation of projects either personally or as requested by the Board;
- follow up of projects, ensuring implementation, and monitoring progress against plan;
- ensuring that top management is aware of progress — and that the organisation knows that top management is aware.

The Profit Improvement Manager will probably not have a very large department, but should have access to the services of others, and some form of functional authority over the traditional improvement agencies mentioned earlier in this chapter. Formal organisational definition is less important to his success than his own abilities and personality, and very positive support from top management. It is not an easy position to fill, and certainly no place for a narrow specialist.

A planned and participatory approach, the third choice suggested above, is a logical extension of the profit improvement manager concept. The methods described briefly here are summarised from the practice of a number of major companies. A more detailed study will be found in Hussey (1974, pp. 217–28). The method has been practised by a minority of companies over a very long period, but is almost unknown outside those companies. Where the corporate climate is ripe for it, this approach can be the most appropriate way of planning and implementing profit improvement, and is therefore a valuable tool with which to combat inflation. It has the further advantages of being fully compatible with a corporate planning philosophy and will also fit well with a programme of management by objectives.

One company has been dedicated to the approach since they began it in the USA in 1946 and claim to save a respectable proportion of their budgeted expense each year through what they term 'methods change'. Other companies have also attained consistent results. The schemes bear names such as OIP (operations improvement programme), PIP (profit improvement programme) and PIU (profit improvement units).

Although each company's scheme has its own unique and individual characteristics, they all have the same underlying concept and principles. Modification of any concept is, of course, desirable to make it fit a particular company situation and the fact that there are differences in application is a healthy sign.

The common characteristics of all the schemes are:

Planned approach. Profit improvement targets are set at the beginning of each period for each area of the company. Performance against target is measured. In this way an attempt is made to alter the random occurrence of improvement opportunities. Because targets in these companies are taken seriously, a genuine effort is made to find more ways of improving.

A discipline. Each system is backed by an internal discipline leading to the orderly identification, analysis and investigation of improvement schemes. This helps things to be done thoroughly, speedily and efficiently.

Coordination. Efforts are coordinated, and in most schemes there are managers designated as responsible for this function. Often managers may be given a coordinative responsibility in addition to their normal duties.

Participation. There is a wide measure of participation in the scheme from many levels in all parts of the organisation. One company goes so far as to write the principles of their scheme into every manager's job description. Profit improvement schemes work within the organisational framework and never usurp the authority of individual managers, yet the whole approach ensures that a corporate view is taken where necessary. Coordination is supported by what might be termed progress chasing. Some schemes are designed to involve all employees; others are only intended to involve managers.

Board support. Each of the schemes has the support of the Board. This gives it driving force and ensures that targets are taken seriously and programmes properly carried out.

Organ of change. The schemes are designed to be important organs of change in the company, and considerable attention is paid to creating the right organisational climate. In this way motivational benefits accrue, which go beyond the profit improvement elements.

Continuum. Although individual projects have deadlines, the total scheme never comes to an end.

These are broad principles. A better idea of how they work can be gained by examining the approach of one particular company.

This firm sees their programme as 'an organised effort to manage improvement on a continuing basis'. The programme aims to identify problems, solve them and make the solutions effective — and, by definition, to produce more improvement opportunities than could have occurred on a haphazard basis.

The intent is realised by working to monetary targets which descend from a corporate target to a goal for each division, usually expressed as an agreed percentage of next year's budgeted expenditure.

The programme is coordinated at corporate, divisional and unit level. Implementation is considered a divisional responsibility, and the link between corporate and divisional coordinators is definite, but informal. It is a close cooperative working arrangement, the development of which is an integral part of the philosophy of the programme. Most coordinators carry on with their normal job; only very few have a full-time responsibility to the programme.

Each coordinator has, with the responsible managers in the organisation, to establish a programme to achieve the monetary goal, and to give some indication at the beginning of the period as to how this will be done. In addition, he has an educational role, spreading the philosophy throughout his unit and teaching the techniques. (This particular company relies heavily on techniques, such as value analysis, which apply a team approach.) He provides an administrative channel for project ideas and a link, through corporate headquarters, with other coordinators.

Every employee is encouraged to submit project ideas to the scheme, one of the coordinators' duties is to prepare a master list of proposals which is considered at regular intervals by an advisory committee of managers from that unit. This committee may adopt, suggest further study, or reject any of the ideas, and has the power to assign responsibility for individual or team action. The power comes from the managers making up the committee. No project can be implemented unless it receives the signature of the responsible managers, thus preserving the normal lines of authority. Both the committee and the coordinator have innovative roles in finding proposals for study, and need not depend solely on ideas from others.

Progress of individual projects, and overall results against targets, are monitored regularly. There are also definite rules on what constitutes a valid claim against a programme target, to avoid double counting and corporate self-delusion. All involved are kept informed of overall progress, as well as what is happening to any specific projects they might have suggested or have worked on.

The underlying philosophy is that there is no limit to the ways in which a company can be improved. The only problems are identification and implementation. The programme cannot come to an end and is as continuous as such normal processes as budgetary control.

It is easy to make a hasty judgement after reading an abbreviated description of what happens in this company, a judgement that 'it would not work for us'. Hasty conclusions are often wrong. The facts demonstrate that this approach to profit improvement can work and does work in a number of companies. It *does* change internal attitudes; it *does* make significant contributions to profits.

One company using a similar approach claims to have produced a saving in costs of £5 million over five years; equally important was a change of attitude in the company. Another believes that it has given them improved motivation and a £500,000 profit improvement. Yet another company finds that their approach has given their organisation a flexibility and enthusiasm for change: they have woven the philosophy into other aspects of the company's management processes, including their personnel and training policies and their views on management development.

In times of severe inflation the motivational benefits cannot be overstressed. Employees need to feel that the company is coping with what they know to be a serious problem, and there is no better way of creating this feeling than involving them in finding some of the solutions.

Each of the four companies I have studied has handled an infinite variety of improvement projects. Some undoubtedly would have been discovered in time by the more conventional approach of the typical organisation; many would have escaped unnoticed. What the schemes often bring is speed of identification, a willingness to apply a new solution and a more imaginative approach both to the identification of problems and the way they are solved. Normal work study, O & M and value analysis experts still have a part to play under the concept, but the emphasis changes.

The company that achieved the £5 million saving handled forty projects during one two-year period, covering such subjects as distribution; hiring of warehouse facilities: the way in which gas, electricity and water were purchased; painting of storage tanks; order handling; and various organisational studies. Lists of successes look very dull and appear little different from those produced by the exponents of the traditional profit improvement techniques, and certainly do not do justice to the full scope of the concept.

The benefits of this continuous profit improvement concept are available to any company prepared to work at it. It is not an economic miracle which occurs as a natural event, but a concept which will only work if the emphasis and interest comes from the top. Like many other management concepts, it is a flower that can only flourish in the right climate: it withers and dies where the conditions are wrong. Top management makes it succeed or fail.

There is no golden rule to indicate which of the many approaches touched on in this chapter is right for a particular company. The minimum that might be done is to examine the techniques and applications in a company and perhaps add a new one. Value analysis for example, can have impressive results in a company which has never used it before. Impressive results might be achieved by introducing a technique into a company for the first time.

Many organisations are in the position of having tried all the techniques, and will be using those that have been proven effective. For these companies significant improvement cannot come from casual methods: they must try a completely different approach if they are to achieve more than they are already doing.

The need to manage improvement on a continuing basis was identified by the company in the example at a time when inflation was relatively low. The British subsidiary of this multinational introduced the approach from their parent company during the mid-1960s, and at the time were concerned over an inflation rate of 4 per cent per year.

For many companies, once general inflation moves above 10 to 15 per cent per year it is arguable that the need is no longer optional, but a matter of simple survival. So far the problem has been looked at only from the self-centred view of the individual business, for this is where the solutions have to begin, and managers are employed to be concerned with the individual firm.

The need for improvement extends to the national economy. Much of British industry has undoubtedly slipped lower in the world's competitive league over the past twenty years. The reasons for this are complex, and the blame must be shared between successive Governments, management, and organised labour. To set the matter right industry requires more confidence, more capital to modernise, cooperation from labour both in accepting innovation and in reducing the time lost in strikes and disputes, fiscal policies which allow it to retain enough capital to make necessary investments, and a Government attitude which encourages (instead of criticising) those who make a profit. Above all, it requires qualities of management. The British motor car industry, now lying well behind the Japanese and Europeans, requires modernisation. It has also had one of the most appalling records in labour relations in British industrial history.

Much of British industry may be in the same position. Yet the Birmingham University work referred to earlier in this chapter shows quite clearly that management is in a position to bring about improvements of a magnitude which could bring a new dimension to British industrial competitiveness. This improvement lies within the power of management itself. It is a task which can no longer be ignored, for the violence of inflation now ensures that there is no hiding place left for those who fail to improve.

References

DUDLEY, N. (1974) 'Note on the scope for improved productivity in industry'; paper prepared for the West Midlands Economic Planning Council, Industry and Employment Committee.

HUSSEY, D. E. (1974) *Corporate Planning: theory and practice*, Pergamon.

The section of this chapter dealing with continuous profit improvement schemes is an adaptation of an article 'Corporate planning: profit improvement' in *The Accountant*, 21 March 1974.

11

Inflation accounting

Inflation has not escaped the attention of the accountancy profession, and the leading thinkers in this field have gradually developed a concept of 'inflation accounting' which has led to changes in accounting practice. The hallmark of respectability has been awarded by the Institute of Chartered Accountants (ICA). What has caused the accountant concern has been the impact of changes in the general purchasing power of money on the validity of historic accounts. Traditionally, the annual financial accounts are prepared on the basis of the historic cost of the transactions recorded, although some companies may periodically revalue certain assets. Items are recorded in the books in terms of the value of the currency on the date when an asset was acquired or revalued, or on the date when a liability was incurred, revenues received or loan or share capital obtained.

> The convention has the advantage that the recorded historic cost is derived from factual monetary transactions, and its use helps to limit the number of matters within the accounts which are subject to the exercise of judgement. However, that advantage is impaired where the purchasing power of the monetary unit used changes significantly over a period of years (ICA, 1973, para. 4).

The fact is that, at even relatively low levels of inflation, transactions recorded this year are not directly comparable with those recorded last year, or those that will be recorded next year. Currency, the traditional yardstick of the accountant, is not the constant standard it is often assumed to be. It is a perpetually shrinking measure. Each year the pound is worth something less than it was a year previously: in times of hyperinflation it may be worth a great deal less. Inflation accounting aims to correct the deficiencies of historic accounting, to take due note of the impact of inflation on the business, and to eliminate unreal paper profits. Just how different results can be when this is done has already been demonstrated in Chapter 1.

Accountants are concerned with presenting a truer and fairer reflection of reality than can be achieved with the traditional approach. This is partly because of their professional duties as custodians of the company's wealth, partly because the modern accountant is deeply concerned with the management decisions which arise from the information he provides. The fact that inflation accounting can lead to different decisions makes it directly relevant to the ordinary manager.

The concept of inflation accounting is as deceptively simple as the concept of double-entry book-keeping. It is to correct historic accounting for changes in the value of money. Double-entry book-keeping, by definition, insists that for every debit entry in the books there is a corresponding credit entry. Both statements disguise the enormous amount of knowledge and technical skill which lies behind modern accounting.

Explaining the concept requires more than an illuminating statement like 'debit is the side nearest the window'. It demands an exploration of the defects of historic accounting, and an evaluation of how the newer approach might be applied as a corrective. Historic accounting has been with us for decades, and its methods have been hallowed by successive generations of businessmen. It is not something to be set aside lightly.

The first problem of historic accounting has already been touched on. It is the fact that accounts prepared on this basis add 'apples and pears', as there is no way in which yesterday's pound can equal today's pound. It has been argued that in a small business this factor is not significant, as managers have sufficient knowledge of the business to adjust the reported results mentally. Much of modern business is not small. Shareholders who are not closely connected with the running of the business are unlikely to be able to make the mental adjustments because of lack of data.

Anything but the crudest of estimates of the effect of inflation are next to impossible to make, because:

(*a*) the rate of change in the purchasing power of money has not been constant

(*b*) the effect of change in the purchasing power of money will vary between companies according to

   I. individual ratios of monetary to nonmonetary items, and

   II. different patterns the course of time in the acquisition of assets, incurring of liabilities and raising of capital (ICA 1973, para. 6).

The 'apples and pears' situation also manifests itself in another problem: the replacement of assets. Normal approaches to depreciation mean that the company underprovides from current profits the amounts it will ultimately require to replace those assets. This is, of course, by no means a new problem, and is complicated by technological changes which have nothing to do with inflation; the company probably would not want to replace its plant and machinery with identical items even if this were possible.

The ICA (1973, para. 17) suggests that there are two classifications of assets, the monetary and nonmonetary items mentioned above. Monetary items consist of those items

> whose amounts are fixed by contracts or otherwise in terms of numbers of pounds, regardless of changes in general price levels. Examples of monetary items are cash, debtors, creditors and loan capital. Holders of monetary assets lose purchasing power during a period of inflation to the extent that any income from the assets does not adequately compensate for the loss.

Nonmonetary items are assets such as stocks, plants and buildings. These are assumed neither to gain nor to lose purchasing power because of inflation alone, as changes in the price of these assets will tend to compensate for movements in the purchasing power of money. (This, of course, is quite different from the problem of replacing depreciated assets.)

The 'apples and pears' result can lead to over-optimistic assessments of revenue, which in turn means that *real* profits are lower than reported. Tax may be paid and dividends declared on profits reported on a historic basis when in real terms the company may have incurred a loss. What on a historic basis may appear to be a handsome appropriation of profit for the future development and growth of the business may be totally inadequate once allowance has been made for inflation. A gross disadvantage of historic costs is therefore that they can lead to a false impression of true profitability. It has been demonstrated that most leading companies would have declared lower profits if these were computed under inflation accounting principles.

Most businesses tend to incur and pay for their costs before cash is received for the ultimate sales. (There may be exceptions, as for example the supermarket which turns goods over for cash before it has settled its suppliers' bills.) Manufacturing businesses carry inventories and pay for their raw materials long before they receive a penny from customers. Labour has to be 'purchased' on a weekly or monthly basis, again long before a sale is made.

Under historic accounting principles, goods which cost £100 to make in January and sold for £150 in December would yield £50 profit. Tax will swallow up part of this, and the remainder will be divided between shareholders and retentions. Assuming 70 per cent goes to the inland revenue and shareholders, only 30 per cent or £15 will be retained. Exactly a year later the company wishes to make the same product again. By this time costs have increased by 20 per cent, which means that to make what used to cost £100, will now require £120. But the company only has its £100 back plus £15 retention, in any terms this can be summarised as a cash flow problem! This example is, of course, grossly oversimplified, and ignores numerous factors which normally come into the profit calculation. These can be safely excluded, since they do not invalidate the basic truth of the example: that a genuine cash flow problem can develop when retention policies are geared to historic accounting concepts.

It would be pleasant if corporation tax were also assessed on inflation accounting principles. Although there have been some minor moves towards this end, it is still a long way away. The Confederation of British Industries (1973, p. 7) argues that 'with the publication of true profit figures it would become clear how large a proportion of real profit is taken by taxation. This would lead to pressure on the revenue to relate assessment to these figures.' If we add to these issues the potential cash flow problems which can arise from paper profits on revalued assets, it is clear that historic accounting methods, although very respectable, have certain defects.

All these factors, taken together, mean that it becomes impossible to compare the true performance of different companies, and that there are gross distortions in return on investment and other ratios used to measure and judge corporate performance.

The approach to inflation accounting which has been proposed by the accounting bodies is the general purchasing power method. This shows the effects on annual accounts of changes in the general purchasing power of money (an attempt to examine true inflation), but ignores changes caused by technology or market factors. This method is not seen as replacing the traditional historic accounting methods (legally it cannot), but as providing a statement of additional information to assist in the interpretation of the historic cost accounts.

The method for converting from the basic accounts to the inflation accounts is relatively simple. ICA (1973, App. 2) presents the theory in three stages:

> 1. Figures for items in the balance sheet at the beginning of the year are converted into pounds of purchasing power at the end of the year as follows:
> (*a*) nonmonetary items are adjusted for changes in the purchasing power of the pound since they were adjusted or revalued.
> (*b*) monetary items are adjusted for any material change in the purchasing power of the pound since the beginning of the year.
> 2. Figures for items in the balance sheet at the end of the year are converted into pounds of purchasing power at the end of the year as follows:

(*a*) nonmonetary items are adjusted for changes in the purchasing power of the pound since they were acquired or revalued.

(*b*) monetary items are, by definition already expressed in terms of pounds of purchasing power at the end of the year, and therefore require no conversion.

The figures for nonmonetary items after conversion need to be reviewed, in the case of stocks, in the light of the test of lower of cost (in pounds of purchasing power at the end of the year) and net realisable value, and in the case of fixed assets in the light of their estimated value to the business. It may then be necessary to make appropriate provisions against the converted figures.

3. The difference between the total equity interest in the converted balance sheets at the beginning and end of the year (after allowing for dividends and the introduction of new capital), is the profit or loss for the year, measured in pounds of purchasing power at the end of the year. This profit or loss can be analysed by producing a profit and loss account including figures expressed in pounds of purchasing power at the end of the year for as many of the items in the company's basic profit and loss account as is desired. In addition to these items the converted profit and loss account will contain a figure, if material, for the net loss or gain in purchasing power resulting from the effects of inflation on the company's net monetary assets or liabilities.

An example of the presentation of the supplementary inflation adjusted accounts appears in an Appendix to this chapter, pp. 133–6.

There is, of course, no perfect inflation index for the conversion of accounts under the general purchasing power method. Criticism can be levelled at any index chosen. Standard accounting practice in the UK is for the basic index to be the consumer price index produced annually by the Central Statistical Office. This has a wider coverage than the more frequently published retail prices index. However, as the financial year end of many companies will not coincide with the period of the consumer price index, this should be adjusted to the correct month through the movement in the retail prices index.

While this approach may be the best available, it has serious difficulties. The first is that the consumer price index, which is in fact a deflator for consumer expenditure in the National Accounts, is subject to retrospective amendment. This means that subsequent changes can make the inflation adjustments incorrect.

The second problem is that there is in fact no general measure of purchasing power. Cowley (1974, p. v) argues:

> It has long been the view of statisticians and economists that no precise meaning can be attached to the concept of the general purchasing power of the pound. . . . A price index expresses the

> relationship between goods and services and the money which is exchanged for them, and cannot be constructed except for a defined class of goods and services: before constructing an index number it is necessary to know the items to be included and their relative importance. Conversely, the value of money cannot be determined without knowledge of who is to spend it and what it is to be spent on. . . . Nor is there any other single price index which is truly applicable to all the items in company accounts.

This qualification clearly reduces the effectiveness of the general purchasing power method of inflation accounting. The alternative of using the most appropriate of officially and privately produced indices to adjust different items in the company accounts suffers from other disadvantages. First, the 'most appropriate' index is not necessarily very appropriate. Second, the element of judgement is increased, making it more difficult to compare the results of one company with another. While the multi-index method may have advantages for the managers within a company, these are overweighed by the disadvantages to shareholders and investors of not being able to judge the inflation-adjusted performance of the company against other possible investments. On balance, the general purchasing power method has fewer disadvantages, particularly when it is considered that much of the incentive to provide inflation-adjusted accounts comes from a desire to meet the needs of those outside the company.

The shortcomings of the recommended standard approach should not be overlooked, and should certainly be considered when the figures are interpreted.

Additional problems arise when the company has subsidiaries or associates outside its home county. The Confederation of British Industries (1973, p. 8) suggests that

> If it is accepted that in the longer term cross rates of exchange reflect the relative degrees of inflation between the countries, in the view of the Committee overseas assets, etc., should be adjusted for changes in local purchasing power indices and converted to sterling at current rates of exchange. On occasions, however, it may be necessary to use the alternative method of converting overseas assets, etc., to sterling at the rates ruling at the time of acquisition, and then, adjusting for changes in UK current purchasing power indices.

It also takes a certain mental flexibility to accept that the profit recorded in the legal accounts, on which tax and dividends have been paid, is not a profit at all in real terms. Some observers suggest that inflation accounting will never be accepted by trade unions, who would always prefer to argue their claim on the basis of historic accounts. Similarly, shareholders are unlikely to be excited about having their dividends based on inflation accounts, for this would mean that most would receive a lower dividend and many would have none at all. It is certainly possible to argue the practical applicability of a technique which, according to one reference (Chambers, 1973) would reduce the profits of 104 of the 137 leading companies.

Exponents of inflation accounting claim that the technique shows companies when they need to increase prices to prevent a fall in real earnings. The CBI report (1973, p. 7) saw this as inflationary, leading to pressure for higher wages. Certainly, when the taxman and organised labour are not playing the inflation accounting game and insist on basing their 'share', on historic accounts, it would be impossible to redress the balance by any reasonably acceptable level of price increases. The other side of the problem is that the ability to apply a price increase depends on the market situation and on any anti-inflation control legislation which may be in force.

Inflation accounting can bring some additional distortions of its own. Chambers (1973) gives an interesting example:

> Companies will profit from inflation accounting if their financial position is poor. This benefit will be clearest when the companies are not engaged in industrial activity. For example, a property company borrows £1 million in January to invest in property. Assuming the rental income just meets the interest charges on the loan, plus administrative expenses, this company shows an extra profit for the year, due to inflation of £85,000. This ignores capital appreciation on the property. The real value of the debt of £1 million has gone down during the year by 8.5 per cent, due to inflation.

Organisations with a strong net monetary asset position will tend to show reduced profits when accounts are adjusted for inflation. This, again, can give a distortion of the true situation. However, in both these situations the inflation adjusted statement will be only a supporting document to the main accounts, and those interested in interpreting results will have both sets of figures at their disposal.

Many of the arguments about inflation accounting presuppose that it will become an influence on management decisions. This, of course, depends on how companies use it. If their only interest is in producing a once a year appendage to the statutory accounts, because this is what the code of practice insists they do, the influence on decisions taken during the year may be marginal. To have any impact on decisions the inflation accounts would have to be fully integrated in the company's management accounting system, which means regular statements at least quarterly and possibly monthly. Only in this way can the data which the inflation accounts try to present have any influence on decisions taken during the period.

Certainly inflation-adjusted year-end accounts could lead to some actions by management, but these are unlikely to be timely. My view is that the company would be unwise to rely on inflation adjustments to lead it to a decision. It must develop a complete awareness to inflation and its impact on all aspects of the company's activities. Inflation accounting can supplement and assist this awareness: it cannot replace it. In other words, the presentation of an annual inflation-adjusted statement by an organisation which pays no attention during the year to any of the factors identified in preceding chapters, is likely to be a waste of time and effort.

The general purchasing power method proposed by the ICA (1973, para. 8)

> shows the effects on annual accounts of inflation only, that is of changes in the general purchasing power or value of money. It does not show changes in value due to changes in other factors such as technology or market pressures, and therefore does not introduce other concepts such as replacement costs or current values. Replacement cost accounting and current or fair value accounting are concepts which can, and do, exist separately from the concept of general price-level adjusted accounting, and they will continue to be discussed and developed for the particular purposes for which they are intended.

Some would argue that replacement cost accounting is an alternative to inflation accounting; a few might see it as a more desirable alternative. In essence, this requires the business to revalue its assets and inventories on the basis of their replacement cost, regardless of their historic costs. Costing systems using this principle would charge to a product the cost of replacing the materials used. The philosophy behind replacement costing is that it is necessary for the business to maintain its physical assets. To do this it needs to generate sufficient monetary assets, which means that its true profits should allow for a 'real' level of replacement, rather than depreciation based on historic costs. In a replacement costing system the fixed assets would be regularly revalued. Depreciation over and above the normal book depreciation would be credited to a special reserve account. Inventories would be revalued at current prices, and any inventory profits credited to a nondistributable reserve.

It is possible to run the business through a replacement costing system which regularly revalues materials at current prices. In normal circumstances this would tend to give rise to apparently higher costs than would have been the case under one of the traditional costing approaches. Unless these higher costs can be translated into higher prices, the result will be to depress profits. Such a system is cumbersome and difficult to operate, and it is more likely that the impact of replacement costing will be analysed in an annual supplementary statement, to be presented with the historic cost results. Some argue that, when this statement is made, monetary items should be adjusted for the change in the value of money, using a general indicator such as the retail prices index. Opinion is divided on this point.

One of the criticisms of replacement costing is that it involves numerous judgements. The valuation of assets is by no means simple, and it is not always practical to obtain a true replacement cost at any given moment. Use will often have to be made of statistical indicators; for example, the wholesale price indices for the most appropriate industry sector when considering plant and machinery. Inventories are usually easier to revalue in principle, since the current price can be obtained. In practice the work involved will ensure that effort is concentrated on the major items, the numerous minor products being ignored. Even with inventories there may be some difficulties, since an enquiry of a vendor about current prices will not always give the same result as a genuine negotiation with an intention to buy. Regularly purchased items will, of course, present fewer difficulties.

As it is with inflation accounting, so it is with replacement costing. The impact on decision-making depends on how management makes use of the information provided, and on its ability to interpret correctly the meaning of the information. Neither technique will solve any problems: either may be used to help management see what the issues really are.

In the final analysis it should be remembered that even historic cost accounting includes many areas of judgement, and profit is no more than a view taken under a set of defined conventions. There is nothing magic in any accounting method. If the newer techniques help managers to take a more realistic view of corporate results they may ultimately prove to have the value that their proponents subscribe to them. For the present there must still be a large question mark over both the techniques and the judgements that go into them.

The importance of inflation accounting (and the difficulty of choosing an appropriate method) was recognised by the Government in January 1974, when a committee of enquiry was set up to study the matter. The committee reported in June 1975, and its report (commonly known as the 'Sandilands report' after its Chairman) was published a few months later (Inflation Accounting Committee, 1975).

Various alternative approaches to the problem were analysed by the Committee, including the current purchasing power and replacement costing methods discussed earlier in this chapter. The report points out that the two methods are not true alternatives, in that replacement costing is only one of several available systems of value accounting available (that is, methods which account in current rather than historic values) and that the CPP Method can be used in conjunction with both the historic cost and value accounting approaches.

The Committee reached three main conclusions:

> First we consider that it is essential that accounts should allow for changes in costs and prices. Secondly we consider that existing accounting conventions do not do so adequately, and tend to present the affairs of companies in a misleading way.
> Thirdly . . . we consider that the most fruitful line of development in inflation accounting is a system based on the principles of value accounting, which shows the specific effect of inflation on individual companies. We recommend that a system to be known as current cost accounting should be developed (p. 3, paras 10 and 11).

Limitations to the value of historic cost accounting under modern inflationary conditions have been discussed earlier in this chapter. The Committee added:

> When prices are changing as fast as they have done in recent years, the usefulness of historic cost accounts becomes so restricted that it is essential to modify accounting practices so as to provide information more relevant to the needs of users of accounts (p. 82, para. 297).

No accounting system can solve the problem of inflation, although it can indicate its effects and help the organisation to take action to mitigate them.

Company profits (or losses) are classified by the Committee into operating, holding and extraordinary, and the recommended current cost accounting method makes full use of this distinction.

> We define an operating gain as the difference between the amounts realised for a company's output (its earnings from goods or services provided) and the 'value to the business' of the inputs used by the company in generating those amounts (p. 20, para. 71).
> We define an extraordinary gain as the difference between the amounts realised for items which do not form part of the company's output and their 'value to the business' at the time of disposal (p. 21, para. 72).
> We define a holding gain as the difference between the measured value to the company of an asset at any point of time and the original cost incurred by the company in purchasing that asset (less depreciation where appropriate). The latter figure will normally be known with certainty and the extent of a holding gain thus normally depends on the method adopted of measuring the value of assets (p. 20, para. 70).

A major implication of this concept is the clear separation of paper profits arising from, for example, inventory revaluation from the real profits of the company. The current cost concept goes even further by arguing that profit for the year should exclude all holding gains and that although extraordinary gains are part of profit they should be separately distinguished from the operating gains.

A second major feature of current cost accounting is that assets and liabilities should be shown in the balance sheet at a valuation which reflects their value to the business. This rarely will be the same as net realisable value, and should be equated with the loss the company would suffer if it were deprived of the asset. In many cases such a value would be replacement cost, but this is not an invariable rule.

Profit under current cost rules requires that depreciation is calculated as a proportion of the value to the business of the asset, and not related to the original purchase price.

Inventory appreciation would be removed from the profit and loss account and taken to a reserve. This would be affected by making a 'cost of sales adjustment' in the profit and loss account, with the objective of ensuring that the 'value to the business' of the inventory is used, rather than its historic cost.

'So far as the profit and loss account is concerned we think that these two adjustments to historic cost accounts, and these two alone, constitute a comprehensive system of accounting for inflation' (p. 162, para. 535).

Advantages claimed for current cost accounting are that it enables intercompany comparisons to be made during a period of heavy inflation on a basis that is meaningful and relevant. The separation of holding and operating gains enable management to be judged on their ability to manage, without the picture being clouded by luck and windfall inventory gains. The approach is 'Evolutionary' in that it contains no fundamental new principles, but builds on practices which, in part at least, are already used by many companies.

The Sandilands recommendations include a timetable requiring (if accepted) the mandatory introduction of current cost accounting by nationalised industries, listed companies and other large companies not later than 24 December 1977. Many practical problems remain to be solved: the taxation problems alone make the proposed date an ambitious one and one recommendation of the report is that a general review of taxation is required which must extend beyond the corporate sector.

The Sandilands report represents the most comprehensive study yet made of the problems of accounting for inflation, and must surely have some effect on future accounting practice.

Appendix: Example of the presentation of a supplementary current purchasing power statement

The example has been prepared in order to illustrate how the figures of a company may be presented in the supplementary current purchasing power statement. It is not intended to be a step-by-step worked example of the calculations involved. The figures are not necessarily typical.

Summary of results and financial position adjusted for the effects of inflation (Note 1)

		Historical basis				*Current general purchasing power basis*		
		£'000 Last year (1)		*£'000 This year (2)*		*£'000 This year (3)*		*£'000 Last year (4)*
Results for the year								
Sales		1,920		2,110		2,190		2,134
Profit before taxation (Note 2)		205		215		175		195
Taxation		82		86		86		89
Profit after taxation		123		129		89		106
Dividends		60		60		61		65
Retained profit for the year		63		69		28		41
Financial position at end of year								
Net current assets		490		556		561		533
Fixed assets less depreciation		558		566		700		714
		1,048		1,122		1,261		1,247
Less: Loan capital (Note 3)	200		200		200		216	
Deferred taxation	39		44		44		42	
		239		244		244		258
Total equity interest		809		878		1,017		989
Ratios								
Earnings per share (p) (based on 500,000 shares in issue)		24.6		25.8		17.8		21.2
Dividend cover (times)		2.1		2.2		1.5		1.6
Return on total equity interest (%)		15.2		14.7		8.8		10.7
Net assets per share (£)		1.6		1.8		2.0		2.0

Notes

1. The figures in the current general purchasing power basis columns were arrived at by converting the corresponding figures in the historical basis columns by reference to the changes in the Consumer Price Index between the dates of the original transactions and the end of 'this year'. The current general purchasing power basis figures for both this and last year are measured in pounds of purchasing power at the end of 'this year'. The Consumer Price Index at the end of this year was 139.3 and at the end of last year was 129. Both figures are based on 19- = 100.

2. *Profit before taxation*
How the difference between profit on a historical basis and on a current general purchasing power basis is made up.

		This year £'000		*Last year £'000*
Profit before taxation (historical basis)		**215**		205
Adjustment to convert to current purchasing power basis				
Stock Additional charge based on restating the cost of stock at the beginning and end of the year in pounds of current purchasing power, thus taking the inflationary element out of the profit on the sale of stocks	**37**		25	
Depreciation Additional depreciation based on cost, measured in pounds of current purchasing power, of fixed assets	**25**		17	
Monetary items Net gain in purchasing power resulting from the effects of inflation on the company's net monetary liabilities	**(12)**		(10)	
Sales, purchases, and all other costs These are increased by the change in the index between the average date at which they occurred and the end of the year. This adjustment increases profit as sales exceed the costs included in this heading	**(10)**		(7)	
		40		25
Profit before taxation (current general purchasing power basis at end of year under review)		**175**		180
Adjustment required to update last year's profit from last year's pounds to this year's pounds				15
Profit before taxation (current general purchasing power basis at end of this year)		**175**		195

3. The loan capital at the beginning of 'this year' amounted to £200,000. £200,000 at the beginning of this year is equivalent in purchasing power to £216,000 at the end of this year (because inflation has been 8 per cent during the year). As the company's liability to the providers of loan capital is fixed in money terms this liability has declined during the year in real terms from £216,000 to £200,000. This reduction of £16,000 in the company's obligation in terms of current purchasing power is included in the net gain on monetary items of £12,000 shown in note 2.

References

INSTITUTE OF CHARTERED ACCOUNTANTS IN ENGLAND AND WALES. Accounting Standards Steering Committee (1973) *Accounting for Changes in the Purchasing Power of Money: proposed statement of standard accounting practice.*

CHAMBERS, A. (1973) 'The impact of inflation on Accounting', *New Society*, 19 July.

CONFEDERATION OF BRITISH INDUSTRY (1973) *Inflation and Company Accounts: An interim report for discussion.*

COWLEY, A. H. (1974) 'Accounting for inflation', *Economic Trends*, no. 250, August.

INFLATION ACCOUNTING COMMITTEE (1975) *Inflation Accounting*, HMSO, London.

12

Action summary

The foregoing chapters have provided an insight into the impact of inflation on business, and suggested a number of practical steps which the individual firm can take to avoid or mitigate the effects of inflation. Ideas can easily be lost among the argument, and in any case have been presented within the chapter structure of the book, which is not the organisational structure of a typical company. For these reasons, this final chapter provides an action summary of more than 100 actions which managers should consider, most of which have been discussed in much greater detail in the main text.

For ease of reference the summary is presented under typical organisational headings. This should not blind the reader to the fact that solutions are often alternatives: for example, a rise in raw material prices may be combated through a major strategic decision, through marketing strategy, by changing production methods or by a new attack from the purchasing function. Choice is not always restricted to one of the options. In many cases the company should be seeking a multiplicity of actions, rather than the one, probably nonexistent, universal panacea.

The most important of all the possible actions is for the company to recognise that inflation brings a structural change to many of the factors which influence profits and that resources should be allocated to the study of its effects. These will vary between companies, and the recommendations of this book can only point to lines of enquiry. Solutions can rarely be lifted from a book without study and modification to suit individual circumstances.

1. Marketing

1.1 Recognise that inflation may bring structural changes to markets, and allocate resources to study and research these changes.

1.2 Reassess marketing prospects of any products affected by severe inflation, considering withdrawal of the product or changes in strategy (such as advertising concepts and promotion expenditure).

1.3 Review longer term plans for all products severely affected and change where necessary.

1.4 Be ruthless in dropping products which cannot contribute to corporate profits and development; do not nurse ailing products in the hope that things will miraculously improve.

1.5 Put a new emphasis on diversification, choosing products which are less inflation prone (remember inflation is unequal in its impact).

1.6 Be aware that competitive positions can change, as inflation will not fall with the same impact on all suppliers to a market. In particular, look out for the challenge of less inflation prone substitutes.

1.7 Look for the marketing opportunities which inflation will bring: such as new product concepts; substitution for other products more adversely affected by inflation; the changed basis of economic decisions which may make certain cost saving equipment viable; or even a new promotional concept which arises because of a change in social attitudes.

1.8 Be more multinational, in terms of marketing and assessing competition, and in terms of the most competitive source of products.

1.9 Take a longer-term view of products, trying to assess the effects of inflation in advance, thus gaining lead time to modify products to improve profits.

1.10 Understand the basis of the company costing system and the implications on profits of volume changes on different costing methods.

1.11 Accept that price reviews may be a more regular feature of business, and that the price policy selected this year will have a significant effect on the price policy for next year. The traditional annual jump in prices when standards are revised can cause immense marketing problems when rates of inflation are high.

1.12 Be suspicious of any marketing projects which require heavy investment and a lengthy time before payback.

1.13 Design promotional material, catalogues and similar items in a way that simplifies the change of price.

1.14 Do not let a necessary price increase be defeated by the inability of the administrative systems to cope with it.

1.15 Be very wary about continuing to market an unprofitable product unless there is firm indication that a change in technology or production costs will restore the position very quickly.

1.16 Consider price variation (or escalation) clauses where the product or market is suitable.

1.17 Ensure that an effective dialogue is established with purchasing so that changed supply conditions can influence marketing thought and development.

1.18 Try to manage the product mix as a deliberate attempt to control the amount of inflation faced by the company (see Chapter 7).

2 Production

2.1 Be aggressive in seeking production solutions in the reduction of cost.

2.2 Examine the alternative sourcing strategies on a worldwide basis. It may be more economic to obtain products from another country.

2.3 Reassess rejected ideas for the installation of new methods or new technology. The economic justification may have changed.

2.4 Be willing to postpone expansion plans, and certainly rescrutinise any which are considered essential. Inflation may have changed the reasons for the original decision.

3 Purchasing

3.1 Consider the organisation of the purchasing department, in particular its ability to influence strategic thinking and the actions of the marketing department.

3.2 Allocate resources to the study of supply markets and the forecasting of supply prices and be aware of the importance of a good base of information about purchases.

3.3 Prepare a purchase plan, to ensure that production, inventories and purchases are related, and that the implications of material and supply prices on production and marketing decisions are properly considered.

3.4 Pay particular attention to inventory, especially if high inflation is accompanied by recession: the so called 'stagflation'. Revise purchase and inventory policies in the light of the purchasing plan and regular monitoring of the situation.

3.5 Ensure that a change in policies is communicated to the clerks who implement it, otherwise old routines will continue to be used, despite management's belief otherwise.

3.6 Analyse purchasing strategy (see Fig. 8.2) and use purchasing considerations as a reason for change in other functions.

3.7 Consider the possibilities of improving the current components of the situation — existing suppliers and existing technologies — by modifying purchase requirements, cooperating with suppliers to develop cheaper methods of meeting purchase needs, or considering other forms of supplier cooperation.

3.8 Seek new suppliers for existing types of products.

3.9 In particular take a multinational view of purchasing, particularly if operating a multinational production or marketing strategy.

3.10 Seek new technology from either existing or new suppliers, developing substitutes with suppliers, or trying to identify substitutes already available from other sources. This may well involve changes in production methods and possible research and development.

3.11 Make one of the aims the use of materials which reduce waste (for example, the choice of pattern on furnishing fabrics will affect the amount of waste for pattern matching).

3.12 Make-or-buy decisions may now be on a different economic basis. Review decisions already made to confirm that they are still correct.

3.13 Ensure that purchasing, through its cooperation in the planning process, receives early warning of proposed product changes, so that the right supplies can be obtained, or if volume is affected, the best use made of the company's bargaining position.

3.14 Consider changing suppliers who will not allow generous credit terms.

3.15 Always question a price increase and be willing to change suppliers where necessary. At the same time, do not force your suppliers into bankruptcy, as this could act against your longer term interests.

4 Finance

4.1 Take particular care to plan cash flows.

4.2 Tighten up credit control policies and procedures, and use all efforts to prevent excessive credit being taken by customers, both because of cash flow needs and the now much higher risks of bad debts.

4.3 Re-examine the terms of trade to give an incentive for early payment, such as charging interest on overdue accounts.

4.4 Take particular note of the impact on cash flow of paper profits, such as inventory revaluation, which are never really available in cash but on which dividends may be paid out and taxes paid (if the 1973—74 concessions are removed at some future date).

4.5 Consider retention and dividend policies on an inflation accounting basis.

4.6 High rates of inflation may bring severe asset replacement problems for some industries, consider a replacement costing approach.

4.7 Question present expectations of future funds, as inflation may make plans invalid. For example, depressed share markets may reduce prospects of more equity participation, or alter opportunities for acquisition and merger through an exchange of shares.

4.8 Delay payment of debts for as long as possible.

5 Personnel and industrial relations

5.1 Expect a period of high inflation to be a period of intense pressure on wages, unless increases are restricted by law.

5.2 Realise that the traditional annual increase is unlikely to last unless accompanied by some form of inflation payment in the following year — either interim payments on an agreed date, or some form of indexation. Inflation at 20 per cent per year will be seen by employees in quite a different way from inflation at 8 per cent.

5.3 Indexation brings greater budgeting problems than agreed interim payments of a predetermined amount.

5.4 Do not place as much faith on annual salary survey data for staff rate fixing as in the past, as high inflation means that it will almost certainly be out of date very quickly.

5.5 Expect a period of trade union militancy, with exceptional pressure from white-collar workers (with unions gaining support because of high percentage wage settlements), and an overriding concern with relativities.

5.6 Tackle the problem of employee motivation in a definite way, as hyperinflation will make this already difficult problem hypercritical. Give management attention to the possibility of applying some of the solutions suggested by the behavioural scientists.

5.7 Plan on the basis that management is in a situation where it may become very difficult to manage wage and salary policies. Consider giving active support to national solutions, such as those proposed by Lord Wilfred Brown or PEP (see Chapter 9).

6 Corporate strategy and general management

6.1 Recognise that inflation has a long-term impact on many aspects of business, and make decisions which take this into account.

6.2 Accept the inequality of inflation, and do not shelter behind sweeping assumptions which assume that all relative positions remain the same.

6.3 Re-examine the company's approach to corporate planning, developing this approach to management in a way that is participative, creative, and carried out in an awareness of external circumstances. Review all planning methods in the light of modern thinking on the subject.

6.4 Formalise the collection and interpretation of business intelligence, including the study of inflation and its effects on markets, political strategy and social trends. Increase the attention given to forecasting these factors, and ensure that the results are considered in planning and decision making.

6.5 Plan on an international basis, taking a multinational view of problems and opportunities. Accept that no company can afford to take a purely parochial view of its activities.

6.6 Re-examine short-term and long-term profit objectives in the light of the rate of inflation, and the probable reduction in real profits that is likely to be revealed by inflation accounting.

6.7 Be particularly aware that hyperinflation poses a severe threat to profits and cash flow, and spend time identifying the effect on your company.

6.8 Review all current strategies, as there may be a need to revise marketing, research and development, production and financial priorities. Some programmes may need to be cancelled or postponed because of changes in prospects, or alteration in the company's expectation of available resources.

6.9 Spend some time looking for the opportunities which inflation will bring.

6.10 Consider capital investment carefully, avoiding expenditure on nonessentials or postponable items.

6.11 Avoid further investment in areas which appear to be becoming the most vulnerable to the ravages of inflation.

6.12 Deliberately seek projects with a cost reduction effect, which may mean re-examining projects previously rejected. New circumstances may make more of these viable, as the benefits of cost savings may increase at a faster rate than the capital cost of the project.

6.13 Seek low investment opportunities for expansion — which could mean seeking licences for new developments, expanding revenue by granting licences for the company's own products, or changing attitudes to partnerships and joint ventures.

6.14 Try to avoid projects with heavy capital requirements and long lead times. Where such projects are desirable, try to divide them into a number of self-contained economic units so that success does not depend on the ability to complete the whole programme.

6.15 Take due note of the time scale needed for some anti-inflation strategies, and ensure that sufficient lead time is built into plans.

6.16 Examine alternative plans under alternative assumptions, analysing the risk involved in corporate plans, and the sensitivity of the plans (and the projects within the plans) to various factors. Be especially careful of strategies with a high risk.

Index